Rhapsody
in Blue

NEIL FITZSIMON

Rhapsody
in Blue

How I Fell in Love with the
Great Chelsea Team of the Early Seventies

First published by Pitch Publishing, 2020

Pitch Publishing
A2 Yeoman Gate
Yeoman Way
Worthing
Sussex
BN13 3QZ
www.pitchpublishing.co.uk
info@pitchpublishing.co.uk

A CIP catalogue record is available for this book
from the British Library.

ISBN 978 1 78531 638 8

Typesetting and origination by Pitch Publishing
Printed and bound in India by Replika Press Pvt. Ltd.

Contents

Prologue

I GO to my mum and dad's every week for tea, and on the way back I drive past some fields at the end of the road that belong to the local school. I see the same thing every week; they are empty. Oh, occasionally you will see some bloke improving his golf swing, but every week I get a catch in my throat and a sense of loss in my stomach that these fields are now deserted and, in a way, unloved and unused. I know they are still in use for organised school games, but these were the fields where I grew up, where we played football at every given opportunity. It was through these fields that I formed friendships that took me into so-called adulthood, where every evening from March to October we would play our own championships, our own private leagues. We would be there at the weekends too. Two games on a Sunday, one in the morning, another in the afternoon after *The Big Match*.

And now they stand empty – a bit like a cherished present that now lies in the dark recesses of a cupboard. But if parallel worlds exist, I know somewhere on those fields it is still the summer of 1971 and I'm still calling for John Clarke every night, then knocking on the houses to see whether anyone's coming down the fields for a game, and Chris Espley is still mishitting crosses much to the fury of the rest of us. And Dave Hyde (struck down by leukaemia at the age of 28) is still as strong as an ox, charging and usually knocking the rest of us out of his way. These friends of mine have now all gone their separate ways, but the field, the edifice, that united all of us still remains. And sometimes when I think it is sad the way we have moved on and that things never stay the same, I know because of that field and its memories, there will always be a part of us that will be forever 16 years of age.

Sometimes, when I watch those old *Match of the Day* reruns of the games from the 60s and 70s, I get a strange feeling that I'm watching part of my youth. Not just the normal feeling of, '*God, wasn't football great back then*', but a thought going around in my head, something like, '*I wonder what I was doing on the day when Ajax won the European Cup in 1972*'. It instantly brings back memories of sitting at home with my mum and dad and my sister, and the way we used to make such an event of any cup final. My mum would always make hot dogs for all of us while my dad would be sitting in his special chair in the corner holding court with his usual two bottles of John Courage, picking out his favourite player and also his scapegoat: some poor unsuspecting soul on one of the sides who would be ridiculed from the first minute of the game until the last.

One of the games featured one week was from December 1964, and it gave me an almost unbearable longing for my childhood. The game had been played on the Saturday before Christmas, and I knew I would have been out there somewhere that day, with my nan, my mum and sister, most probably dragging them around the shops seeing if there was any chance of scrounging a last-minute present from them. And most probably on that Saturday night I would have watched that very game – and being so close to Christmas, my sister and I might have been allowed a glass of Emva Cream as a treat, and I would have been almost drunk with joy at the fact that school had come to a close and I'd be able to do my very favourite thing – stay in and do absolutely nothing apart from play with my soldiers, read books and listen to my records. That Christmas I got *A Hard Day's Night* and played it until it was practically worn away.

I know when you look back it is hard not to surround everything in a golden aura, but there is no doubt in my mind that this was a more innocent era than the one in which we live now. In fact, I believe that decade and part of the early 1970s were the last great years to be living in this country, before we turned into 'little America', and the greed inspired by Margaret Thatcher and her cronies transformed a lot of us into money-grabbing automatons. The sense of longing that I feel for those days also brings on a sense of pity for those too young to have ever known what it was like to be a kid back then. In fact, I could say that up until July 1969, when my grandfather died, I had enjoyed an idyllic childhood and for that I feel blessed. Even through my grandfather's death, my mum and dad still managed to give my sister and I a holiday on the Isle of Wight, which to this day remains one of the most bitter-sweet memories of my life. And at the end of that summer when, on reflection, that sense of total security finally ended, my love affair with Chelsea Football Club started.

In my late teens I would go out into the garden on summer evenings and look up into the sky and imagine that where the inky blue clouds met the peach-coloured sunset, was where all the days gone by and the days yet to come, lived. And that was where my nan and grandad first met and all of my family, now scattered far and wide, were hop-picking again in the fields of Kent. And that was the place where all my future girlfriends lived. All these people I had yet to meet and all the mates I had then and those I would lose in the future – that was where we would all meet up again – and all of us would have that same passion for living that the years to come would erase from us. And the air would be as fresh as the breezes that blow in from the sea. And the smell of candyfloss would remind all of us of a time when anything seemed possible – even the impossible – and that we would all live forever. I think the sadness in a lot of us is that we've become myopic and self-possessed, not realising that what is truly essential is not our polarised little lives, but the innocence that lies within our hearts.

Chapter 1

An Innocent Abroad

IT WAS during the 1968/69 season, when we lived in the Elephant and Castle, that I started going to Chelsea on a regular basis. I'd been a few times that year, with my dad, but that wasn't enough for me. For one thing, I didn't want to sit in the stands. As far as I was concerned, there was only one place to be, and that was in the Shed. Even though the prospect of standing there scared me half to death, I was determined that that was where I had to be.

Eventually, I persuaded my mum and dad to let me go on my own. Seeing as I was only 13, and the trip across London was a long one, they were a bit concerned for my safety. As for my nan, she was beside herself with worry. When I left on the day of the game, she hugged me tightly and told me, 'Don't talk to strangers ... don't do this ... don't do that ...' For a split second I almost decided not to go as the guilt that she was laying on me and all the worry that I was going to cause the family, made me feel like a selfish little shit. But at that age, that feeling lasted for about five seconds.

Finally, I was off! And with the aid of my trusty little underground map, I found my way to Stamford Bridge. The opponents that day were Sunderland. After the two sterile draws I'd watched earlier in the season with my dad, I was hoping for something better. I wasn't let down. The whole day was a fantastic experience. The Shed, to me at the time, seemed the wildest and most exciting place I'd ever been to. As for the game, Chelsea destroyed Sunderland 5-1 with my hero, Bobby Tambling, getting four of the goals. I could hardly wait for the final whistle. I was practically bursting with the need to get home and tell my mum and dad all about the game.

That night, my mum, dad, nan, grandad and my sister listened to endless retellings of the day's great events. My nan even cooked my favourite tea – bacon, chips and tinned tomatoes – to celebrate my 'homecoming'.

'There,' she said, 'get stuck in! You're home now and I'm sure your dad will take you again soon.' There was a silence. My dad looked guilty. My nan said, 'What's going on?'

'Actually, Mum,' my dad replied to my nan, 'I've said he can go again next week if he likes.' My nan looked crestfallen and said to my dad, 'Johnny, how could you!' My nan was too shocked to speak to me. Me? I was triumphant. I was on my way!

Chapter 2

The Hidden Menace

BY THE time Man United visited the Bridge in March 1969, I'd been to about half a dozen games on my own. My mates at school were dead jealous that I was going to all of these matches by myself. Two of them finally pressured their mums and dads into letting them go with me, telling them that 'Neil will look after us – he knows what he's doing'. Talk about the blind leading the blind.

So, on a grey, overcast March day, Kevin Dalton, Jeff Stagg and myself set out on the journey to the Bridge. Kevin was a Man United supporter: a forerunner I suppose of all those cockney reds you get today. Though to be fair, his family were from Northern Ireland, where you do tend to get a lot of people supporting United. And as his dad had always followed them, it was pretty much determined from birth who he would support. Kevin's dad, by the way, was one of those mad Irishmen who could sink about 20 pints a night and still manage to get up for work the next day as fresh as a daisy. Kevin idolised George Best and, especially, Willie Morgan. He tried to emulate their way of running and dribbling with the ball and I must say that at the level we played at, he was an excellent player. He also possessed his dad's wild streak and had a quick, fiery temper that got us in and out of a lot of scrapes through the years.

As for Jeff Stagg, he was a very quiet, thoughtful type who was at ease with his own company. It came as no surprise to me to find out many years later that Jeff had ended up working as a bus driver. Although Jeff supported Liverpool and loved football, he didn't seem the type to rough it in the Shed and I was surprised when he said he'd like to come along. I think he wanted to prove to himself that he could go through with it. I've no doubt that after the day's events, he wished that he'd stayed firmly at home.

We got to the ground at about 12 o'clock – nice and early to get a good view. When the gates opened at half twelve, it was already apparent that this was like no other home game I'd ever been to. The streets around Stamford Bridge were packed. Queues for the turnstiles went all the way back to the tube station. Man United, as they are today, were the biggest draw in the country. Although this United side had been in a state of gradual decline since their European Cup win the year before, they still hadn't started on the enormous job of rebuilding the side, and a lot of the current players were now coming to the end of what was a glorious career. It was to be Matt Busby's final season in charge and, apart from the holy trinity of George Best, Bobby Charlton and Denis Law, their team basically wasn't up to much. Not to put too fine a point on it, they were crap. In fact, Chelsea had annihilated them 4-0 at Old Trafford earlier in the season. Before that game, United had paraded the European Cup and then Chelsea proceeded to completely rain on their parade. What a laugh! In the next five years their decline continued and United were relegated in 1974, much to the amusement of the rest of the football world. And though they bounced back a year later, it wasn't until 1993 that they finally won another championship.

Getting into the ground that March day was terrible. The entrance to the turnstiles was narrow – and the crowd huge – the result being that you were virtually carried along on a seething mass of humanity towards the turnstiles. It was pretty frightening. Jeff and Kevin looked shocked at the way people just shoved and pushed their way forward. It was the survival of the fittest. The relief you felt when you were through the turnstiles and finally managed to get into the ground was brilliant.

The first thing you had to do was find your way down to the front to get a good view. I reckon there were at least 30,000 in the ground by one o'clock and by the time the game kicked off, there were 61,000 people crammed into Stamford Bridge. The atmosphere was electric. The whole of the North End was a cauldron of the red and white scarves of Man United. The Shed were taunting them mercilessly. Just before the kick-off, Kevin opened his jacket to reveal a Man United rosette pinned to his jumper. That's one thing you don't seem to see now at grounds – and this one was pathetically naff. In the middle of the rosette was a horseshoe with 'Good Luck Man United' written underneath it. Me and Jeff pissed ourselves. Kevin said he didn't see what the joke was.

The game kicked off on a pitch that resembled a beach. It makes me laugh when you hear the modern-day pros moaning about the state of the playing surfaces they face every week. In those days the players were just as talented, tougher and got on with it. After 15 minutes, Chelsea went one up through David Webb. United were pinned back in their own half and the pressure was relentless, so it came as no surprise when Chelsea scored a second goal, when Ian Hutchinson, that season's major discovery, hit an angled drive past Alex Stepney. With United reeling and taking a right battering, I still wasn't shocked when, despite all of this, United pulled one back on the stroke of half-time. So, it was 2-1 to Chelsea.

Kevin was convinced that United would pull it back. And though I put on a brave face, I'd lost count of the times I'd seen Chelsea lose two-goal leads. The one bright spot at half-time was the news that Arsenal were losing 1-0 to third division Swindon in the League Cup Final. A deafening cheer went up from both sets of fans. Surely Swindon couldn't hold on?

So, the second half started and again Chelsea were pushing United back. This pressure finally paid off when Bobby Tambling scored a brilliant goal to put Chelsea 3-1 ahead. It really was a great goal. As Tambling ran on to a through pass, he hit the ball first time and beat Stepney. The execution of the strike was so sweet and perfect – the ball flew past Stepney before he could move. The noise in the Shed was so great that it seemed as though the terraces were shaking beneath your feet.

And there stood poor Kevin. A splatter of red in a sea of blue and white.

As for Jeff, he was just wide-eyed at the whole spectacle he was witnessing.

Chelsea continued to dominate but with ten minutes left, United pulled themselves back into the game when they were awarded a penalty which Denis Law duly dispatched. Those last few minutes seemed to go on forever, but Chelsea held on, to my relief, to win 3-2. In all fairness, Chelsea had dominated the majority of the game and in my eyes, the scoreline flattered United.

Kevin took it really well. We even shook hands! What a pair of twats!

As for George Best, well he hardly had a kick. Ron Harris stuck to him like glue. In fact, years later, Best revealed that he always hated playing against Chelsea, as Harris followed him everywhere. He said that at half-time, in the changing rooms, he half expected to find Harris sitting next to him.

The scenes outside the ground were unbelievable. You could hardly move for the crush of people trying to get to Fulham Broadway. That, coupled with fights breaking out between rival supporters, meant the situation was total chaos. In those days at the Bridge, they used to let the away fans out at the same time as the home crowd. The result was a battlefield – at the tube station especially as the away end was right on top of it. I can clearly remember seeing a United supporter, his face battered and bleeding, trying to buy a hot dog, only for the vendor to tell him to sod off as his blood was dripping on to the onions!

When we finally got on to the platform at Fulham Broadway, we pushed our way to the front of the crowd – that was our first big mistake. When the train pulled in, the crowd surged forward. I lost my footing as the doors opened. As I was pushed forward, I cracked my shin on the step into the train. Looking back, I was lucky that I wasn't crushed to death. It was a wonder in those days that there wasn't a tragedy earlier than the one that happened at Ibrox 18 months later. Inside the train, it was hot and stifling. We were packed in like sardines. You could hardly breathe. Kevin and Jeff looked to me as if to say, 'What now?' They must've been bloody joking. I was just as scared as they were. To our relief, the train emptied out when we got to Edgware Road. Then we made our next connection to get the train to Euston Square – thankfully, this train was virtually empty.

As we came up out of the station to make our way to the main Euston terminal, a kid stopped us on the stairs and said, 'If you're Chelsea, I wouldn't go up there – there's loads of Man United waiting to kick your head in.' With the total bullshit and bravado of youth, we announced that we'd take our chances. He just said, 'Suit yourself', and disappeared down into the station.

When we got on to the street, there didn't seem to be anyone around. Obviously, a wind-up. But then, all of a sudden, three United supporters jumped us from a doorway. They were about three years older than us and one of them decided that I was to be his victim. He actually started to strangle me with my scarf. As he was behind me, and a lot stronger, I could do virtually nothing. Kevin, meanwhile, was holding his own with one of the others, whilst Jeff was pressed up against a wall – crying. I wondered what the hell was going on when the United supporter that was strangling me, let out a cry of pain. He suddenly let go of my scarf. I turned round to see Kevin's Man United rosette pin stuck in his leg. Kevin had plunged it in, up to the hilt. I think the other two United supporters were as shocked as us as their mate was hopping around and crying in absolute agony, not knowing what to do with himself. We quickly made a run for it. To our horror, we saw that they were running after us. Well, two of them were. The one with the rosette pin in his leg was hobbling behind them. As we ran on to the concourse at Euston, at about 100 miles per hour, we made for a bunch of coppers and the three United supporters, glaring at us from a distance, finally gave up the chase. Despite all that, we didn't leave those coppers' sides until our train turned up. Even the sight of the United players arriving at Euston to get the train back up to Manchester did not persuade Kevin to leave the sanctuary that the police provided, in order to get his heroes' autographs. I did see Bobby Charlton and Denis Law gladly giving theirs – as did the rest of the United players. The only exception was George Best, who told one kid to 'fuck off!' I suppose he might have thought that it was Harris, still following him!

As the train pulled out of Euston, we breathed a sigh of relief. The journey home was uneventful, apart from one thing. We stopped at Wembley and picked up some Arsenal supporters who'd just seen their team lose 3-1 to Swindon in the League Cup Final. The sight of their stupid, miserable faces is one of the most abiding memories I've carried through the years. All in all, it had turned out to be a great day – Chelsea beating United and Arsenal losing a cup final. Brilliant!

Chapter 3

Nerves

WHEN IT comes to watching the Chels, I have always been a nervous wreck. OK, there are times when I seem to take everything in my stride. But when it comes to the crunch games, I still go through my usual routines – things like saying to myself, if we can get through the next ten minutes, that will only leave X amount of time to go. It is a superstition that can be wiped out in a split second, but still I persist with my routine.

I remember a game against QPR in March 1974 at the Bridge. To be truthful they had given us the runaround and were leading 2-1, when Bill Garner (yes, Bill Garner), who they had struggled against in the aerial battles, scored two looping headers to put us 3-2 up. A couple of minutes after the restart, I started having images of how I was going to rip the piss out of my mate, Quentin, who was a die-hard QPR fan. All of the snide comments that I could think of were flowing in my mind. Then Stan Bowles shimmied past two of our defenders and smacked the ball high into John Phillips's net. I learnt that day to keep my counsel whenever Chelsea had a good result against one of my mates' teams, because football has a way of biting you back, hard.

One game that stands out from the 1969/70 season is the home game with Derby County in October 1969. Derby had just been promoted to Division One, and they were led by the great Brian Clough, with Dave Mackay, who had been considered surplus to requirements by Spurs, as their captain. They had taken the First Division by storm. Only a few weeks before, they had annihilated Spurs 5-0 at the Baseball Ground, with Mackay in imperious form against his old club. I felt sick on the train going to Euston, worrying about the game and, just to put a tin lid on it, I actually vomited in the toilets when I reached London. Why? That's hard to explain. You see at the age of 14, the Chelsea players were my heroes and the thought of them losing at the Bridge was a disaster to me. I worshipped the very ground that they walked on.

I remember it was a really sunny, early-autumn day and Derby were doing so well, but our form had been indifferent after an injury-ridden start to the season. I'd made my way on my normal journey, around the corner from Euston, to Euston Square. Why Euston Square? I do not know. Another example of superstition and luck must be involved somewhere. It was always the train to Edgware Road, change at High Street, Kensington for the train to Fulham Broadway. To this day, I still remember the thrill of seeing the floodlights towering above the train as we pulled into Fulham Broadway. The ascent of the stairs and finally you were there. Turn left, and you were at the old club shop next door to the Stamford Bridge café. You were then hit by the aroma of hot-dogs, onions and burgers. The scent of cigarette smoke, the smell of manure from the police horses, as in those days, there was a heavy presence of coppers way before the kick-off.

I always used to go in the Ovaltine entrance, which led to the terrace in front of the tea bar, which was located between the Shed and the West Stand benches. And then, there it was, Stamford Bridge, in all of its sparkling glory. People always say, and they are right, that the sight of the pitch is breathtaking, and on this beautiful early autumn day, the pitch in all its resplendent beauty, with the grass a beautiful, verdant green, was indeed just that. To this day, the first sight of the pitch still evokes a powerful feeling within me.

The sweet smell of raw onions emitted from the tea bar where grey frankfurters floated in what looked like pond water. Then there was the bloke in the white coat selling peanuts, followed not far behind, by the hot chestnut seller. Quickly, I used to buy my Golden Goal ticket and then sit on the terraces reading my programme, whilst listening to Pete Owen's pre-match spin. Whenever I think about this game, in my mind I always hear Lou Christie's, 'I'm Gonna Make You Mine'. It's funny how music triggers a memory in your brain that takes you straight back to the place and time. It's the same whenever I hear Bob and Marcia's, 'Young Gifted and Black'. I have a vivid memory of the 2-2 home draw with Burnley in the fourth round of the FA Cup in January 1970.

I seem to recall that the Derby game was goalless in the first half. But Derby had been brilliant and it seemed that we were just about holding on. Midway through the second half, the inevitable happened and Derby scored with John O'Hare finding the back of the net. Chelsea were looking a bit ponderous in attack. In fact, I checked the line-up recently and Peter Osgood was on the bench, with Alan Birchenall playing up front as a lone striker. In the next month or so, Dave Sexton would give up trying to turn Ossie into a midfielder and put together one of the greatest pairings up front in Chelsea's history – Ossie and Hutch. Hutch was the perfect foil for Ossie. A case of the rapier-like skills of Osgood and the brute force of Hutchinson. It was a partnership made in heaven. It was also around this time that 'The Liquidator', by the Harry J Allstars, was first played at the Bridge and became the anthem that it still is today.

With Derby leading 1-0, Chelsea, as per usual, started to dominate the game and suddenly Derby were on the back foot. The pressure finally paid off. With about 20 minutes left, the ball was squared to Nobby Houseman, who proceeded to smash it, first time, into Derby keeper Les Green's net. By the way, Green was only 5ft 8in tall, but even a six-footer would have had no chance, as Nobby's shot rocketed into the top corner. Chelsea then started to turn the screw but, as so often happens in football, with 12 minutes to go, Derby caught us on the break. The Derby winger, Alan Hinton (before he started wearing the white boots) had been a thorn in our side all afternoon. His cross from the right was met by Kevin Hector to put Derby 2-1 up. This all happened down at the north end of the ground. So, with only just over ten minutes to go, my worst fears had been realised. Then Chelsea pressed again and with eight minutes left, John Hollins hit a low drive off both posts and into the Derby net. 2-2! I would take a draw. Please, God, don't let Derby score again! In fact, it was Chelsea who nearly won the game in the last few minutes when Birchenall put the ball over the bar when it would have been easier to score. And then the ref blew the final whistle. I was relieved that at least we hadn't lost. Derby had been a real handful, but we had shown great character to peg them back twice.

And all of the day's events I could relive that night, as the BBC cameras had been there for *Match of the Day*, which in those times was a real bonus, as *The Big Match* and *Match of the Day* were the only way to see your team on TV for most of the season. In those days, it was easy to shut someone down in an argument about football, unlike today when every Tom, Dick and Harry armchair fan has a view. No, it was easy. If one of my mates said, 'What happened to Chelsea yesterday?' I would reply, 'Did you go?' The answer was always in the negative. With a withering look directed at the hapless idiot, the conversation was closed. I remember playing down at the fields and in between games, I said to my mate John (who was a Spurs supporter – I know! But he was my best friend), 'Who have you got next week?' He replied, 'We've got Crystal Palace.' All of a sudden, one of the kids, not a regular down the fields it must be said, chipped in with, 'What are you talking about? What do you mean, *we*? You're not part of the club. You just support them.' John's face flushed with embarrassment, then I chimed in with, 'We go every week. We pay their fucking wages, you twat!' And so, I'd slung it straight back in the snidey little git's face. The strange thing is, we never heard anything from that mug again.

Chapter 4

The Two-Goal Lead

THE TWO-GOAL lead. What a contradiction in terms that is. A scoreline that suggests the game is over, only for that illusion to be destroyed when your opponents pull a goal back. The swagger and confidence seem to vanish into the ether. And all of a sudden, that unassailable lead is under dire threat. The first time this happened to me watching Chelsea was the home game against Wolves in the 69/70 season. My sister and I watched as John Dempsey and then Ossie put us two up. Ossie's goal can still be seen on YouTube. The elegant way he picked up the ball, just outside the box, and curled a brilliant shot past Phil Parkes (not the West Ham and QPR goalkeeper) into the back of the net, seemed to put the game to bed. As far as I can remember, we fully deserved our two-goal lead, but then, with ten minutes left, Wolves got a goal back. Suddenly, all of our sweet, sweeping passing game seemed to evaporate and we were hanging on. What happened next seemed inevitable and our worst fears were realised when Wolves equalised with a few minutes left. A game that was firmly in our hands had been totally turned on its head. By the time the final whistle blew, we were the team that were glad to hear it. It was a horrible, empty experience to see the Wolves supporters celebrating under the old North Stand. I hardly spoke to my sister, Elaine, on the journey back to Euston. She seemed frightened to say anything to me. I was, and still am, a bloody nightmare if Chelsea have had a disappointing result. To rub it in, all the Wolves players were in the main hall at Euston, waiting for their train back to the Midlands. Elaine and myself, in our blue and white scarves, must have looked so miserable because Derek Parkin, the Wolves full-back, came up and said, 'Cheer up, you two. It's not the end of the world.' A nice gesture, I suppose, and something that would not happen in today's game; but at that moment, it did seem just like the end of the world.

Though the draw against Wolves was deeply disappointing, it was nothing compared to the fourth-round cup tie that year against Burnley. After a slow start to the season, things had improved drastically for us by the time January came around. We were third in the league and one of the favourites for the FA Cup. Although the game against Burnley looked winnable, and we were expected to progress, it must be remembered that despite being a mid-table first division side, Burnley had caused us many problems in the past. In the April of 1969 we had lost 3-2 at home to them after leading 2-1. Ralph Coates, their star player, had run us ragged that day. Coates, with his Bobby Charlton comb-over, was instrumental to everything they did. In fact, Burnley were so reliant on him that they would still print his name in the programme when he was injured. Later on, he joined Spurs, but Coates was a northern lad, and he was a fish out of water in London and failed to make any impact at Tottenham.

At half-time in the game against Burnley it was still 0-0. Again, Coates was their key player. We finally broke the deadlock on the hour, when John Hollins scored with a low shot along the ground. Almost instantly, we scored again through Ossie, whose header at the far post from Alan Hudson's clever cross put us 2-0 up. It looked like that was it, as we took total control of the game. That was, until Mr Coates seemed to take the game by the scruff of the neck. With ten minutes left, he put Martin Dobson through to score, to make it 2-1. Yet again, it was the Wolves nightmare happening in front of our very eyes. Now we were hanging on. With five minutes left, a stray pass by John Dempsey went straight to Coates, who ran at our defence and then played a clever pass straight into the path of Dobson, who made no mistake to equalise. There was a deathly silence around the Bridge. It was a depressing sight to see Burnley celebrating at the North Stand end. When the final whistle blew, it had all ended in a 2-2 draw. My sister and I had an argument, what about, I don't know. Something pathetic, I imagine. We stood there like a couple of idiots pushing and shoving each other. All this took place beneath the shadow of the tea bar. It was a horrible, horrible feeling. I was totally obsessed with us winning the cup. It was a monkey on our back. It was all about the cup. Yes, winning the league would be great, but that was for northern teams.

At school that year, I had done a drawing of Chelsea parading the FA Cup around Wembley. Our art teacher, Mr Horsefall, (a Leeds fan) sniggered when he saw it. 'I always knew you were a dreamer, Fitzsimon, but that is bloody ridiculous!' he laughed. How sweet, that just a few months later, I would discover that revenge is a dish best served cold.

The replay against Burnley was to be played on the following Tuesday at Turf Moor. In the preceding days, I must have been the epitome of the difficult teenager. I moped my way around the house and was in no better mood at school. Of course, the game wasn't on the TV in those days. *Sportsnight with Coleman*, which was shown on a Wednesday night, was the only chance to see any midweek football. I don't even know if there was live commentary on the radio, so I had to sit there, through TV programmes that played out in front of me. What they were about, I have no clue. All I could think about was how we were getting on against Burnley. Surely, this couldn't be the end of the dream for yet another year. Another year of having to live with the fact that we had bloody well lost to Spurs in our only appearance in a major cup final at Wembley. Then, after the news that night, the boring BBC voice announced, 'Here are tonight's football results.' I hid behind the settee, my sister covered her face with her hands, not daring to look. Oh, the relief when I heard my dad say, 'Blimey! Chelsea won 3-1.' I danced around the front room. My sister was jumping up and down. Yet again, the Blues had taken us to the brink of despair, but that had now turned to joy. The dream was back on.

Chapter 5

Street Football – A New Beginning

STREET FOOTBALL was, at the time, a way of life for me and my mates – but it no longer exists. Then, football was not only played at club grounds on Saturdays and Sundays, but also on council parks and even stretches of grass outside people's homes any day of the week. The 'No Ball Games' signs often became one of the goalposts. The rivalry in these games was fierce and partisan. With no referee involved, it was usually no holds barred.

The street team I played for was called Avenue and had been formed three years before my family moved from London to Hertfordshire. Avenue were a closed, cliquey bunch and it took me quite a while before I became one of the lads. I was told on more than one occasion about a legendary game against a team of Catholic Irish kids. Avenue had been 7-1 down but had managed to come back to force a 7-7 draw. The story became longer and more tedious every time I heard it.

There was another story they often told me about a game against a team of Pakistani kids who were then new to this country. Avenue were awarded a penalty and as Chris ran up to take the spot kick, this Pakistani kid appeared from nowhere and tackled him and cleared the ball. Our lot were totally bemused as the Pakistani kids actually tried to play on, not realising what a penalty was.

We always struggled against the Pakistanis, mostly because we were a fair-minded bunch of kids. However, there was another street team consisting of a right bunch of herberts. All cropped hair, Ben Sherman button-down shirts and Doc Martens. Not to put too fine a point on it, they absolutely kicked the shit out of the Asian team. There was no PC around in those days and their attitude towards the Pakistanis was a mixture of contempt and racial bigotry. Mind you, that's not to say that they took it easy on us either. I cannot remember us ever getting even a draw against them.

Unlike the other teams we played, we had our own kit, which we had to buy ourselves. First it was green shirts with yellow sleeves and then we switched to orange shirts with blue shorts at my instigation. Like most neighbourhood teams, we were a rag-tag bunch of kids who could play, mixed with people who would never get into a Sunday league team, let alone a school team.

When I first went down to the fields, I was told about big Kev. He was, I was told, tough and hard. My reaction to this was, '*Who is this tosser?*' The first time I played against big Kev, he cleaned me out with a tackle from behind that lifted me off my feet. I ended up falling on top of him. I was so shocked, I put my hands around his throat and tried to strangle him, shouting, 'What the fuck are you playing at!' Needless to say, from that moment on, we became firm friends.

We also had another kid called Bug. Why? I do not know. His mum insisted that he wear gloves in the winter, an act which was strictly taboo and girly in those days. He was also accident prone. Like me, he was a Chelsea supporter, so I felt a kind of affinity with him. One day, he tried to copy the Charlie Cooke drag-back. The result was, that he trod on the ball, fell on to the bone-hard pitch and broke his arm. On another occasion, when he was playing in goal, he tipped a fierce shot on to the inside of the post, only for the ball to bounce straight back into his face, resulting in a bloodied nose. The final act for Bug was quite sad. He was no player, but on this occasion, he was getting the better of a kid called Gary, who played for the district team. Much to Gary's annoyance and disgust, Bug kept on taking the ball from him. The rest of us found this to be very amusing. With Bug being left-footed, he had an advantage when defending against a right-sided player. As the light faded that evening, once again Bug robbed Gary of the ball. With that, out of nowhere, Gary chinned him. Bug was very skinny, in fact you would say, puny, and he went down like a pack of cards. The rest of us were shocked. It was one of those moments where everything went quiet, not a word was said. Gary went and picked up his holdall, got his clothes and walked off. We went over to Bug, who had a cut lip and yet again, a bloodied nose. Nothing was said. Poor old Bug trudged home that night alone. He never ever played on those fields again.

Though I've loved supporting and watching Chelsea over the years, with all the highs and lows that go with that experience, there is nothing that comes close to playing football yourself, no matter what level you play at. It's only when you stop playing that you realise how much you miss the thrill of the week-in week-out, involvement.

I honestly believe that watching football is a poor second to playing.

Although I played in various Saturday and Sunday league teams, it was the days spent playing down our fields that I look back on with the fondest memories. I suppose there was a main core of eight of us, supported by the waifs and strays that you seemed to pick up each week. They used to turn up, ask if they could have a game – some stayed for a week, some a couple of months, and then they slowly drifted away, soon to be replaced by someone else who would then, for a while, become part of the fold. In fact, that was the way I started off on those fields.

When my family first moved from London's Elephant and Castle, I went to school on the other side of Hemel Hempstead. Hence, I didn't know anybody in our street. All my school-mates lived too far away for me to join them in their nightly games. What was worse was that from my bedroom, I could see these kids playing down at the fields. I can clearly remember the longing I felt, wanting to join in. This desperate situation went on for about three months – a lifetime at that age. My dad said to me, 'You'll just have to pluck up the courage and go down there and ask if you can play.' I think he was sick and tired of me moping about the house every night. I'd found Hemel to be totally different to London, where it was easy to find a game of some sort every night as the parks used to be full of kids playing in various games. Out in the sticks it seemed to be a different story. There appeared to be something called a 'clique', a word I had never come across in London. A private game, where involvement seemed to be by invitation only.

A couple of days later, feeling really nervous, I somehow found the courage and made my way down to the fields. I clearly remember standing behind one of the goals, feeling like a right lemon. Keeping goal that night was John Clarke, who went on to be one of my best friends. We got talking and he said he'd have a word at half-time. My choice of person to approach was inspired as John's family were from north London and I felt an empathy with John and his family from day one.

Anyway, at half-time, he kept his word and grudgingly, they said I could join in. Thus began friendships that lasted for the next 20 years. Though to me, those days spent down the fields were the most magical, in hindsight, they only lasted about five years in total. But what great times they were. And though the Sunday games were brilliant, it was the spring through to autumn and the lighter evenings when things really took off. In fact, the winter months were fraught with peril. If the Sunday game was rained or snowed off, that was it for the week! Five days of going to school with nothing to look forward to in the evenings. But once it got round to March, we'd slowly come out of hibernation. I would start the sequence off by calling for John. We would then knock for Bug, the Kleiner twins, Dave Hyde, John Davenport, Steve Webb, Gary Knapp, Chris Espley and Dave Banton and, with a few stragglers joining in, we usually had a five- or six-a-side game every evening. Then along came the summer months and when the school holidays started, everything went into overdrive. Our normal day would start with a game in the morning followed by tournaments of Subbuteo in the afternoon, finally rounded off by another game in the evening. After we'd finished playing, we'd all congregate and sit on the wall outside John Clarke's house and, as dusk fell in those heady summer months, with the sweet smell of people's bonfires burning away, we would talk our talk at the wonder of what we were discovering every day. I should imagine a lot of it was complete and utter nonsense, but at 14 years of age, your universe is very small, and I wonder now if you ever really see things with the same crystalline beauty that you do when you and the world you lived in were very young.

Chapter 6

The Gear Kid

MY BEST mate down at the fields was John Clarke. He was three years older than the rest of us and we all kind of looked up to him. Away from playing football, John was quiet and unassuming, but put him on a football pitch and things turned decidedly dark. He had the unusual habit of making a noise with his mouth that sounded like a motorbike revving as he closed you down, and when it sped up, you just knew you were in trouble. In fact, some of our opponents christened him 'the gear kid'. He also bore a passing resemblance to a combination of Catweazle and Rod Hull.

On one occasion he didn't speak to me for a week after he had raked his studs down the back of my leg. It was bloody agony, so I turned around and gave him a slap. The other kids were horrified that I had dared to lay hands on John, the almighty John. Towards the end of the following week, I phoned him, on my mum's advice. She said to me, 'Even though he's older than you, be the bigger man.' We quickly made up and I'm glad to say, never fell out again.

In the summer of 1971, John perpetrated perhaps his greatest crime at those fields. In a kick-about game one evening, he overran the ball as he was bearing down on goal. Bants, who was one of our mates, was in goal. As Bants rushed off his line to pick up the loose ball, John hurled himself through the air like a kamikaze pilot. With both feet raised, he crashed into Bants's left shin. My view of this was clear as day as I was running behind Bants, just in case John actually managed to put the ball past him. The sound of the crack of the bone was like a pistol shot. Bants was writhing on the grass in complete agony. The screams were horrific. A couple of us then went to get Bants's dad and the three of us managed to carry him home. I shall never forget the sound of his sobbing.

Unbelievably, the game continued. In the 1970s, not even a bullet to the head would have stopped the game. It turned out that Bants had broken his leg in two places, a really nasty injury that put him in hospital. Although John lived almost opposite Bants, he never once visited him in hospital. To my knowledge, he never even said sorry. John was a good mate of mine but when it came to football, there was something of the night about him.

Chapter 7

Gentleman J.D.

THE BIGGEST anomaly down at those fields was J.D. Not to put too fine a point on it, he was totally hopeless at football, yet he loved the game with a passion. Because it was always difficult to get 11 players for our games against other street teams, J.D. who, of course, had bought the strip, often made up the numbers. He was, it must be said, a complete spoon foot. But also, he was so nice and gentle that having a go at him would have been like stealing money out of your gran's purse. He always played with a hankie up the sleeve of his shirt, in case his nose became runny. If the opposition scored a good goal, J.D. would stand there and applaud them. In fact, on one occasion when J.D. was marking me, he stood off me, allowing me to turn and hit the ball over my shoulder into the far corner of the goal. With this, J.D. clapped and said, 'Oh, well done!' Gary, who was the goalkeeper at the time, said to him, 'Why don't you try marking him instead of applauding him!'

In one game against our bitterest rivals (who, unlike the Avenue, didn't have a name, but came from a nearby neighbourhood), we were losing 1-0 with about 15 minutes left. We had hammered them for most of the second half in search of an equaliser. This eventually came with about ten minutes left. As so often happens in football, we then went on to score again almost immediately, to put us 2-1 up. There were just a few minutes remaining. We had dominated the game and fully deserved our lead. With seconds to go, they got the ball out wide, their winger sent in a soft, hopeful cross and our goalie came out shouting, 'keeper's ball'. Unfortunately, J.D. took no notice of this. He stuck a knee out and diverted the ball into our net. Anyone else would have got a right royal bollocking. But as J.D. stood there, saying, 'Oh dear, oh dear,' it seemed to us that we could never be so unkind to a bloke that loved the game, but was a walking disaster when it came to playing it.

But, without question, J.D.'s crowning glory came in a game amongst ourselves one Sunday morning. It had hammered with rain the previous night and the pitch was totally waterlogged. Chris got the ball and glided past J.D. No surprise there. But hold on, J.D. gave chase! As he ran behind Chris, he managed, accidentally of course, to clip Chris's foot. After that it was like watching Laurel and Hardy. Chris went flying through the air, unable to stop his momentum. He dived head first into what resembled a paddy field. He ended up face down in a pool of water and filthy mud. The rest of us laughed so much, it hurt. Chris stood up, absolutely covered in mud from head to foot. He looked like the *Creature From the Black Lagoon*. But there was no need to worry. J.D. was on hand to help. He quickly offered his hankie to Chris, as if that would help clear up the mud and grime that Chris was covered in. From then on, J.D. was christened 'Norman', after one of the principal thugs from the brilliant but vicious Leeds team of the 1970s, Norman Hunter.

I think J.D. became quite proud of that nickname. Another strange thing about him, again totally at odds with his character, was that when we started getting into cars, most of the lads bought what we could afford – you know, an Austin 1100 and such like. One weekend, we were going to a wedding down in Wiltshire. I could hardly believe my eyes when J.D. came round to pick me up. He was driving a bright yellow Triumph Stag. It seemed so incongruous that this mild-mannered, conservative bloke was driving a car that was deemed at the time to be one of the best cars to drive to pull girls.

But in the end, inevitably I suppose, J.D. became a bank manager and got married to one of his cashiers. J.D., like a lot of the boys I played football with, was a Watford supporter, as they were the local club to where we all lived. When I first started going down to those fields in 1970, I was Billy Big Bollocks. I supported the cup winners and one of the most glamorous teams in the country. In 1971, my stock rose even higher with the European Cup Winners' Cup win. However, by the late 70s, I was on the receiving end of murderous piss-taking, as Chelsea lurched from one disaster to another and, while they were yo-yoing between the second and first division, Watford were making their mercurial rise from the depths of the fourth division to the top of the first. I had no choice but to take all their jibes firmly on the chin.

One footnote to my recollections of J.D. is that in the late 70s we were playing a game amongst ourselves. On this particular day, J.D. was playing on the opposite team to me. I managed somehow to volley a shot at point-blank range into J.D.'s stomach. I suppose the ball must have hit him at about 60mph. He collapsed to the ground with snot pouring from his nose and spittle dripping from his mouth. He was unable to even get a breath. And then to finally cap it all, he vomited. Luckily, after a few minutes, he was OK, even though his eyes were streaming with tears. I felt terrible. It was like I had killed Bambi. Of course, all the others made sure that I was never allowed to forget this, and it was often brought up in the following years.

Chapter 8

Battering the Bumpkins

BY MARCH 1970, I had been playing football down on the fields for about a month. I recall that the evenings were light but, looking back, I thought I must have been mistaken. Light evenings in February? So, I decided to Google it, and yes, there it was – double British summer time was introduced between 1969 and 1972. So, I was relieved to find that my mind wasn't playing tricks on me. Although I knew the boys who played down there by their Christian names, I was hardly one of their mates. No, I had not been allowed into the cliquey inner sanctum. Most of them supported the local club, Watford. So, who did we draw in the semi-final in 1970? You guessed – Watford. They were full of it down at the fields, boasting of how they were going to 'do' Chelsea. Their reasoning was that they had knocked out Liverpool in the quarter-finals, 1-0, and they thought that we would be their next victim. But Chelsea were a different prospect to Liverpool that season. Bill Shankly was in the process of rebuilding a new side, whilst Chelsea were at the height of their powers. The local rag was full of it, 'Hornets on the March' and other tub-thumping headlines. The tickets for the semi-final were going on sale at nine o'clock on a Sunday morning at the Bridge. This was quite a trek for me and my sister. In those days, although there was a Sunday service on the trains, it would have meant getting up at the crack of dawn to get to the Bridge for nine o'clock. The better option was my dad's cunning plan. He worked as an accountant in an office with two old dears who were lifelong Watford supporters and he got them to arrange membership of the Watford Supporters' Club, which made me and my sister, Elaine, eligible for a ticket for the semi-final. Segregation had yet to be introduced into most grounds. Also, the match was being played at White Hart Lane, which would have made it even more difficult to split the fans. So, on a bitterly cold Sunday at the end of February, we made our way to our local station to get a train to Watford's Vicarage Road ground. Though we were going undercover, like two fifth columnists with our two membership cards safely tucked away, did we feel guilty? Not for a minute. We walked away with our tickets, revelling in the fact that the stupid bumpkins had fallen for it. Imagine, they had just sold two tickets to the enemy.

In the week leading up to the semi-final, my mum calmly told me that one of her friends she went shopping with was the mother of John Williams, the Watford full-back. I was struck dumb. The way she told me was as understated as saying 'your tea is ready'. John's mother said that he was a bit nervous about marking Osgood (with good reason). I gave my mum a message to give to John Williams's mother, 'Tell him you're going to get bloody murdered on Saturday.' My spite knew no bounds. My sister, Elaine, and I had arranged to travel on the train to Euston from Hertfordshire with some of my school mates who were Chelsea as well. At the local station, the platform was crammed with Watford supporters, with their banners and gold and black scarves. The train was also packed with Watford fans and in the sea of gold and black were myself, Elaine, Robbo, Alan and Jeff, wearing our blue and white scarves like badges of honour. Though I was again nervous about the match, I just couldn't see Watford being too much of a problem. We were third in the First Division and they were 18th in the Second Division and, in Ossie and Hutch, we had the best striking duo in the league that season. After all, we had missed Manchester United and more importantly, Leeds, in the draw for the semi-final, so we would never have a better chance of getting to Wembley.

On the journey to Euston, we went past Wembley's twin towers, with flags flying proudly at the top of the stadium. It always thrilled me to see that sight – and I thought, '*if we get through today, that's where we'll be playing in April*'. Like the Champions League in the present day, the FA Cup was our holy grail. We had never won the cup, much to the amusement of other supporters. There was even a musical song of the 1930s that took the piss out of that fact, called 'The Day Chelsea Won the Cup', alluding to the fact that other strange things would be happening in the world before we would get our hands on that elusive trophy.

When we arrived at Euston, we made our way on to the concourse and into the main hall. Again, we were surrounded by hundreds of Watford fans. Amongst these were my new mates from the fields, in their black and gold scarves. Though I knew them by name, I stared straight through them, for today, they were the enemy. Chelsea were allocated the Park Lane end that day, which was the Spurs end. It was great to see a mass of blue and white replacing the knuckle scrapers who usually stood there.

I remember the Watford supporters chanting, 'Come on Chelsea!' which to me seemed like the ultimate death wish. Right on cue, a blue wave hit the Watford end and Watford were driven off pretty smartish, on their toes.

We were all standing on the corner of the Park Lane end that adjoins the Shelf. There were 55,000 there that day, and whilst it was packed, it all seemed pretty safe. And then things turned decidedly dark when loads of latecomers started pushing from the back. It seemed that quite a few of them had had one pint too many. All of a sudden, we were caught in a crush. Everyone started to panic. The weight and pressure of people cascading down the terraces was bloody terrifying. We were all caught on a crash barrier and for a moment I could not even move my arms. Then one bloke standing next to me started screaming as his arm was pinned against the barrier. I managed to push back against the crash barrier and created a gap and got my sister and myself under the barrier. As soon as we got under the barrier, a crushing wave of humanity buckled the steel structure. I managed to get Elaine down to the front, right in front of the corner flag.

Whilst all of this was going on, the game had actually started. A St John Ambulance bloke got me over the wall on to the running track by the side of the pitch. I then started to lift my sister over the wall to safety, when I got shoved by a copper who told me to stand back. I looked round to see Alan Hudson behind me, taking the first corner of the game. I turned back round to help my sister up and over the surround. Unfortunately, whilst doing this, I heard Hudson take the corner, I glanced over my shoulder and saw Webby slide in at the far post to put us one up. I then proceeded to almost drop my sister back into the crowd, but fortunately a copper grabbed her and helped her on to the side of the pitch. The police then put us into the Park Lane end as, although it was packed, none of the mayhem had spread that far. I then saw one of my mates, Alan, being passed over the heads of the crowd. He had apparently fainted, either from the pressure of the crush or out of sheer bloody terror. The kid who had been screaming whilst trapped at the barrier was lying by the side of the pitch as the ambulance man attempted to put his arm in a sling. His arm was in a shocking state, turning a horrible shade of blue and black and there seemed to be a swelling in his forearm which I presume was caused by the broken bone. But that was how it was. Going to football in those days could be a visceral experience.

By half-time, with the game level at 1-1, we had been moved to the terrace on the Shelf. Alan, who had now recovered from fainting, asked if we would like some tea from his flask. When he opened it, it had been crushed through the pressure of the crowd and there were bits of the inner lining floating around in the tea. So, in light of that, we declined his kind offer. During all of this, after 11 minutes, Watford had equalised when Terry Garbett hit a hopeful shot towards Peter Bonetti's goal. The ball bounced up off the pitch, which resembled a sand dune, and hit the back of our net. The whole of the Watford end went mad. Despite always fearing the worst, on that day I just couldn't see them beating us. I just had this feeling that that year – like I did during the 2012 Champions League run – nothing was going to stop us. I remember being really very relieved that I'd got Elaine to safety, as my mum and dad were quite worried about me going to games with my sister. To people of my generation, Ibrox and Heysel and of course, Hillsborough, came as no shock. It was, as the saying goes, an accident waiting to happen. I've watched the footage of that semi-final against

Watford on Chelsea TV many times, and try as I might to spot myself, I am just out of shot when Alan Hudson takes the early corner. However, when Brian Moore, the ITV commentator, is going through the team line-ups on the TV, you can clearly see that something has gone very wrong in that corner of White Hart Lane.

Ten minutes into the second half and the Blues retook the lead after Alan Hudson brilliantly switched play with a ball out to Nobby Houseman, who looked up and found Ossie with a pinpoint cross. Mrs Williams's son's worst fears had been realised. After that, the heart seemed to go out of Watford as Nobby added a brilliant solo third goal. Then Hutch blasted home a drive on the turn to fire in number four. A neat one-two between Nobby and Hutch led to the former side-footing the ball past Mick Walker for Chelsea's fifth. It should have been six but, mysteriously, the ref disallowed a stunning Ossie goal for absolutely no reason. I've watched that goal many times on TV and it still remains a mystery as to why it was disallowed.

So, we were going to Wembley. Another chance to finally lift our first FA Cup. Now all that stood before us were Leeds or Manchester United. I hoped it would be Manchester United, as they were a fading force, but in my heart, I knew there was only one team we were destined to face – and that was Leeds United.

Chapter 9

Hutch

TO THIS day, Ian Hutchinson remains one of my favourite Chelsea players of all time. He joined in the summer of 1968 for £5,000 from Cambridge United. I think, initially, he was bought as a full-back, but it seems that during that summer Dave Sexton converted him into a centre-forward.

I first became aware of him when my mate told me about his debut against Ipswich at the Bridge. He told me about this new forward who had an unbelievable long throw-in that caused such chaos in the Ipswich defence that Bill Baxter, their centre-half, actually headed one of Hutch's long throws into his own net. My mate also told me that he was all arms and legs and really put himself about. Though he was only a bit-part player in the 68/69 season, he did become more involved towards the end of that year and weighed in with some important goals. But that year, our main two strikers were Bobby Tambling and Alan Birchenall, with Ossie still playing in midfield. I was totally obsessed with Bobby Tambling and even wrote him a letter. Unbelievably, I was sent a copy of Bobby's testimonial brochure with a really nice message from him. I treasured those words of his for years.

However, early in the 69/70 season, which we had started really slowly, we were hit with a string of injuries to our first-choice players, including Tambling and Birchenall. Hutch had got his chance and he grabbed it with both hands. When Dave Sexton moved Ossie back up front, the partnership with Hutch clicked almost straight away and they became the best striking partnership in the country that season, with Ossie netting 31 goals and Hutch scoring 26, as we finally brought home the FA Cup for the first time in the club's history.

They really looked the part as well. Ossie was swagger personified and Hutch was all power and long sideburns. (Oh, how I dreamed of growing whiskers like that!) Where Ossie was elegance and guile, Hutch was the raw-boned battering ram who took so much punishment for the cause. My sister fancied Hutch. She went with me to the 1-1 home draw against Crystal Palace in August 69 and was hooked straight away. That season she went with me to most of the games. After one match she said she wanted to go to the club shop (the megastore – it was not!). She then proceeded to buy a poster of Hutch and he duly took his place on her bedroom wall alongside the likes of Paul Newman and Steve McQueen.

Little did we know that that season would be the pinnacle of Hutch's career at Chelsea, culminating in his brave, near-post header against Leeds in the 1970 FA Cup Final at Wembley. It was a goal that snatched a draw for us when we were only four minutes away from defeat. And of course, we will never forget his 40-yard-long throw which led to David Webb's winning goal in the Old Trafford replay against Leeds.

Hutch started the 70/71 season really well, netting in the Charity Shield against Everton, and then scoring a brace against Derby in the opening league game. It was in the winter of that year that his long list of injuries started. He broke his arm in a game against Nottingham Forest, an injury sustained when he laid out the Forest centre-half, Sammy Chapman. Was Hutch sent off? No chance. This was the 70s. But his injury problems really started in February 1971 when Hutch tore a cartilage in the away game at the Dell against Southampton. A minor injury by today's standards, but at that time it meant six months out. Subsequently, he missed the Cup Winners' Cup run that led to that brilliant night in Athens where we beat Real Madrid 2-1 to bring the first ever European trophy back to Stamford Bridge.

Over the summer of 71, his rehabilitation seemed to be going well and it looked like he would be back in the new season. But in a reserve game against Swindon, he collided with their keeper which resulted in a double fracture of his leg. And so, Hutch was out for the season. Chelsea quickly moved to sign Chris Garland from Bristol City and inexplicably sold Keith Weller to Leicester to soften the blow of the £100,000 fee paid for Garland. It was galling to watch Weller in the following years, blossom into a star for Leicester. Add in the fact that he also went on to play for England, and the decision to sell him became even more painful. Though Garland scored some vital goals for the Blues, he never formed the lethal partnership with Ossie that Hutch had. Although we reached the League Cup Final that year, where we lost unexpectedly 2-1 to Stoke, worse news was to follow just one week later.

I remember picking up the evening paper on the Friday following the Wembley defeat, only to read to my horror, that Hutch's leg had been broken again. This time, it was a stress fracture; an injury he sustained whilst running up and down the terraces at the Shed end, which on reflection was not perhaps the wisest decision on behalf of the physio department. And it was something that in today's game would be unthinkable, in a world where sports science is now endemic. Once again, Hutch was back to square one.

All went well during the summer and he seemed to be making progress. However, the club were taking no chances and decided to spend £80,000 on Southend's Bill Garner, after knocking his club out of the League Cup. Southend were a third division club and whilst Bill Garner was good in the air, sadly he was no replacement for Hutch.

In the period that Hutchinson was out injured, amongst Chelsea supporters he had become the panacea to all our troubles. We were all sure that once he was back and reunited with Ossie, things would start to improve. In fact, there were already signs of the decline that ended up with us being relegated in 1975. Unlike the 1970 cup-winning side, there was an air of vulnerability about the team now.

We got off to a good start in the 1972/73 season but by the autumn results began to dip. In one particular game against Southampton at the Dell, where we completely outplayed the home team, we still managed to find a way to lose 3-1. Then, in early December the news started to spread that Hutch was nearing a return. Finally, on 22 December 1972, Hutch was named in a front line consisting of Ossie, Hutch and Bill Garner for the home game against Norwich. I have never known such an outpouring of love for one player. The chorus of 'We want Hutch' rang around the ground. In fact, some bloke who was standing behind me and my mate Steve Gallagher, said, 'Bloody hell, it sounds like a protest march for homeless rabbits.'

Bill Garner opened the scoring to put us into the lead midway through the second half. Then Hutch's moment came as he hit a low shot past Norwich keeper Kevin Keelan to put us 2-0 up. Norwich hit back almost immediately after a mazy run by Jim Bone to make it 2-1. But this was Hutch's day. He sealed his comeback with a brave header for Chelsea's third. Finally, he was back. The fire and spirit we had lacked seemed to have returned. Hutch left the field in triumph at the final whistle.

Four days later Norwich were back again for the League Cup semi-final, first leg. This time there was no fairy tale as Norwich beat us 2-0 and went on to the final to play Spurs. Hutch then continued to play in the next few games, but in January 73 his luck ran out again in the home game against Derby, which is mainly remembered for Ossie's brilliant curling shot which earned us a 1-1 draw. It was also notable for that incredible miss by Derby's Roger Davies in the last few minutes, when he managed to trip over his own feet after rounding Phillips. This was the game that saw Hutch limping off with a knee injury. This time his cartilage had gone.

Yet again, Hutch was out for the rest of the season. Chelsea limped home in 12th place that year and now the writing was on the wall, with money being lost hand over fist due to the new East Stand not being opened. Consequently, there was little money left to reinforce the squad. Hutch was back for the start of the 73/74 season, but we made a terrible start and soon found ourselves rooted to the bottom of the table. After a good run in the late autumn and early December, we picked up and at one stage were eighth in the table. Then we lost 2-1 to Leeds at the Bridge and the bubble burst. Within weeks, following the 4-2 Boxing Day collapse to West Ham at the Bridge, a game in which we had led 2-0, the vitriol that existed between Sexton and the star players erupted. In January 74, Ossie and Alan Hudson were placed on the transfer list for being disruptive influences. It seemed at one stage as though things might be settled between the manager and his rebellious stars, but the board decided to back the manager. By March, Ossie had been sold to Southampton and Hudson had moved on to Stoke City. It was a mortal blow. During this time, Hutch was actually placed on the transfer list as well, most probably because he was great mates with Ossie and must have made obvious his displeasure at the situation.

On 13 March 1974, I went to the home game against Burnley. It was an afternoon kick-off during the working week owing to the miners' strike, which had dragged on for weeks, meaning no floodlights could be used for night games. In front of a pitiful crowd of under 9,000, Hutch scored one of his greatest goals for the Blues when he thumped a 25-yard volley into the net. Steve Kember's cross was headed clear by a Burnley defender straight to Hutch, who was standing 25 yards out. Hutch met the ball full on the volley and his thunderous drive almost broke the back of the net before Burnley keeper Alan Stevenson could move. It was a goal of awesome power and showed just what Chelsea and England had been missing through Hutch's terrible run of injuries. This goal sealed a 3-0 win. Hutch was then quickly taken off the transfer list and, although he made occasional appearances, the injuries were taking their toll. He scored another brilliant goal against Stoke in October 1974, in a League Cup tie at the Bridge when he crashed a shot home on the turn, with the ball hitting the underside of the bar and bouncing over the line. A brief, yet brilliant, vignette of what we had lost when his injuries began to take their toll.

In January 1976, just before the home FA Cup tie against Crystal Palace, at the age of just 27, Hutch was forced to call it a day. I felt numb when I read this – that one of my favourite players had finally succumbed to the debilitating injuries he had sustained over the last five years. In fact, it had seemed to come out of the blue, as Hutch had actually scored a few weeks earlier in the fourth-round cup tie against York City. Sometimes I wonder what he would have been like in Eddie McCreadie's promotion-winning side of the 76/77 season. He would most probably have taken the role of the veteran leading all those young players that made that team so brash and exciting.

Instead, I think that Hutch found adjusting to life away from football difficult. In those days, there wasn't the money around that there is today and pros had to face up to a normal working life. Hutch embarked on a few different paths. For a while, he was the commercial manager at the Bridge. Then he and Ossie opened their own restaurant/bar, which in retrospect was most probably not a good idea, owing to their legendary reputation down the King's Road. Before I forget, there is one other little-known fact – Hutch appeared in a John Collier advert (the men's outfitters) in 1971. I only saw it once on the telly, but it was the usual stuff served up at that time, i.e. footballer is chased down the street by dolly birds who spot him in his new suit. Sadly, there is no happy ending for Hutch. He passed away at the age of just 54 in 2002 after a long illness. Sadly, he was joined four years later by Ossie, his great mate. So now they are both reunited forever.

In the end, what did we lose? Well, we lost one of the bravest players to ever wear the shirt. There have been more technically gifted players at the club, but when it comes to a big heart, he stands alone.

Chapter 10

Nobby

WHERE DO you start with Peter Houseman? Or Nobby, as he was called. And, let's be honest, also the rather cruel nickname of Mary, something he had to live with during his whole Chelsea career. I'll put my hands up and admit that I was guilty of calling him that.

It must be said, Nobby was integral to the cup run of 1970. After one game in which he scored, my dad said to me, 'I see your mate, Mary scored again.' I felt shame-faced. The trouble with Nobby was that next to the Holy Trinity of Cooke, Hudson and Osgood, who were the epitome of the glamorous King's Road, Nobby looked like a customer service assistant at the NatWest. With his short back and sides and his quiet unassuming manner, he was always the first player to come in for stick, which at times, was merciless. However, recently, I watched the 1970 cup finals against Leeds on Chelsea TV and, my God, what a clever player Nobby was. Hardly any passes went astray as he quietly got on with his job in midfield.

He was also a great crosser of the ball, in an era when a winger was a specialised position. In today's game it tends to be overlapping full-backs who put the crosses in, so they often lack that skill (Ashley Cole is not included in this tirade). Nobby scored vital goals in the 1970 cup run including two in the semi-final against Watford and, of course, the first equaliser in the Wembley final against Leeds. But it was his goal in the fourth-round replay against Burnley that was perhaps the most vital. We had blown a two-goal lead at the Bridge and on a cold, murky night at Turf Moor, Nobby struck the equaliser with 17 minutes to go. This inspired us to go on and beat them 3-1 in extra time, with Nobby getting his second goal of the game before Tommy Baldwin grabbed the killer third goal. The rest is history. He also scored the vital opening goal against Brugge in the 1971 European Cup Winners' Cup quarter-final where we came back from a 2-0 first leg defeat to beat the Belgians 4-0 after extra time. Sadly, Nobby's life came to a tragic end when he, his wife and their two friends were killed in a road smash in March 1977 at the age of just 31. I would like to think that Nobby is up there with Ossie and Hutch, who have also made that journey to a blue heaven. So, here's to Nobby – gone, but never forgotten.

Chapter 11

Mouth Almighty

WHEN WE moved to Hemel Hempstead in 1969, I knew no one. My school was on the other side of town, so I would often go out on my bike in the hope of joining in one of the many games that kids used to play back in those days. I was desperate for football. It was a good thing that it was fairly easy to get yourself involved in what was known as a pick-up game. On this particular day I got involved in a game in some local garages that were at the back of some council houses. At these games, if you skied your shot, it usually ended up in someone's back garden. In fact, one day, some bloke actually climbed up on to his garage roof and burst our football. We just stood there with a look of dismay on our faces. Anyway, on this occasion, the kids were all about my age, 14 or so, except for one boy who must have been about 18. He was a big fat lummox with a mouth to match. After the game, he said he was impressed with us and would we be interested in joining a new team he was forming? Of course, all of us jumped at the idea. Here was an older boy telling us he wanted to form a new team with us as its founding members. He then suggested we go back to his house to have a meeting. My God, how naïve you are at that age. He could have been a serial killer, taking us back to his gimp dungeon. It could have been just like that scene in *Pulp Fiction* where Bruce Willis was taken prisoner by two redneck perverts. Add in the fact that he was twice our size in height and width, and indeed, we must have been mad.

How best to describe the home of that tub of lard? Well, it looked just like him, scruffy and dishevelled. There was the pervasive aroma of mincemeat and onions, stale cabbage and countless fry-ups. The sofa looked like it had taken a battering as I should imagine, the lummox Andy, wasn't the only heavyweight in his family. I could clearly see the stuffing almost exploding through the well-worn, shiny cushions. All in all, it was a bit of a tip but matched somehow the down-at-heel, unkempt appearance of our host. None of his clothes looked like they fitted him properly, I suspect because as well as growing taller by the day, he was also growing wider. His shoes were worn right down, flat at the heels, perhaps not only because they had seen better days, but also because they had been crushed by the immense weight bearing down on them. I found out some time later from his peers that Andy was in fact a pathological liar and teller of tall tales, and that we had just been the latest victims on a very long list. Yet for us, for those brief few hours, we had believed every word he said.

We listened to two hours of complete and utter bullshit. I can't remember what the team was going to be called, but I'm sure it would have been his choice and not ours. He then made one of us captain and proceeded to tell us that he came from a football family. His surname was Stenhouse. Therefore, it was his grandfather who had

founded Stenhousemuir FC. We were all very impressed.
I'm afraid at that age you believe any drivel that is spouted.
He then told us that he knew someone at the Herts FA
who could get us into one of the Sunday leagues. It all
sounded so great. Suddenly, one of his adoring audience,
'the newly appointed skipper', asked him a question.
Without warning he went mad and exploded, 'What do
you fucking mean, keep on asking me questions!' He then
stripped the boy of the captaincy and dropped him from
our first game. Yes, that's right, dropped from a team that
only had four players, against opponents that didn't exist.
At the end of the meeting, he took our phone numbers
and addresses and said he would be in touch with news.
To this day, I still haven't heard from him.

Chapter 12

The Cup at Last – Part 1

THE FA Cup Final at Wembley on 11 April 1970 is an occasion enshrined in the minds of all Chelsea supporters of that generation. The two weeks leading up to the final were torture. Some days I was full of hope, only then to remember that it was Leeds United that we were playing in the final. Leeds, the devil's own team. Technically brilliant but infected with an evil streak that has blighted their reputation through the years.

But surely this time it would be our turn? Losing to Spurs in the 1967 final had been bad enough, but to lose two cup finals within the space of three years was something I didn't want to think about. Surely this time we would get our hands on a prize that had eluded us all through our history? We were the most glamorous team in the land and due to the fact that fans of other clubs, to a man, despised Leeds, somehow we had become the neutral's favourite. How could Ossie, Hudson and Cooke end up on the losing side? It was unthinkable.

At home, my sister and I persuaded my mum and dad to allow us to put up the official Chelsea team photo for the FA Cup Final, above the fireplace. I can still recall that picture, with 'Chelsea 1970' emblazoned on it in a typically trendy 1970 typeface. That photo stayed on that wall above the fireplace in our front room for about four years. By the time it was taken down, due to re-decorating, the glory days of 1970 were nothing but a distant memory.

Because we had bought every programme for the home games, even those games we'd missed, my sister and myself were lucky enough to get tickets through the voucher system that was included on the back of club programmes in those days, just on the off chance that your team might make it to Wembley.

I remember receiving our tickets for the final with a mixture of excitement, hope and crushing fear. During the week leading up to the final, I remember watching a BBC TV programme called *Quiz Ball*. It was football themed, with Barry Davis of *Match of the Day* being the host and question master. I suppose, in a way, it was a forerunner of *Question of Sport*. Both teams consisted of two of the brightest players from opposing football clubs. This being cup final week, it was, of course, Chelsea and Leeds. I'm not sure, but I think our team consisted of Johnny Hollins and the Cat, Peter Bonetti. As for Leeds, I'm pretty certain one of their representatives was Johnny Giles. I fully expected Leeds to start bullying Barry Davis and feigning injury (this is a joke). Chelsea were triumphant – mind you, I think we'd have had a harder job beating two orangutans. Surely this was a good omen? Yes – but then again, no. Perhaps we had used up all of our luck beating the two Leeds knuckle-scrapers.

Like most things that you dread, it was the waiting that was the killer. I can't remember a thing about school that week, leading up to the final. I can't even remember whether I went down to the fields to play our usual evening game. I should imagine I would have been down there, as the pressure of just sitting at home thinking about Wembley would have driven me out of the house to the fields for a game – something to take my mind off Saturday.

I clearly remember going down to those fields on the morning of the final. A game was underway, but I didn't join in, as my legs felt strangely weak. I think I was in need of some human contact. You see, for the rest of my mates down those fields, this was just a normal Saturday. Quick game in the morning, get home in time for the televised build-up to the final, which featured *It's a Cup Final Knockout* and *Meet the Teams at the Hotel*. They would also film the finalists' coach journeys on the way to Wembley. My mates would then sit down to enjoy the game on the TV – something that I would not be doing that afternoon. It still amuses me today when, in the middle of a tense, exciting match, they cut away on the TV coverage to see the reaction on the faces of the fans. For some reason, you always get some moron grinning madly into the camera, even though his team are losing. Safe to say, that easy come, easy go attitude was not something shared by me and my sister.

When we arrived at Wembley Central, it was alive with Chelsea, packing out the trains from Euston. The walk up Wembley Way was incredible, where everything seemed dwarfed by those massive twin towers. I remember the *Daily Express* were selling a special cup final souvenir edition. With every copy came a paper hat emblazoned with, 'Win or Lose, Up the Blues'. I bought the paper but ditched the hat. Losing today was not an option. I'd only been 11 when we had lost the 1967 final to Spurs, but in my child's mind I consoled myself with the fact that at least we had got to the final. This time, defeat was unthinkable.

Chelsea were allocated the Tunnel End that year at Wembley and though there were thousands of Chelsea fans all around us, there were still plenty of people standing nearby who didn't seem to give a toss about the result of the game. It was nothing short of a disgrace that the two finalists only received 16,000 tickets each; the rest of the 100,000 crowd was made up of FA cronies, hangers-on and transient spectators. Years later, the team I played for on a Sunday even received a ticket themselves to raffle. You must realise that in those days this was *the* game in club football, and I mean worldwide, and to deny the fans of either club was nothing short of shameful.

Now, I can tell you that I remember that game vividly but there are some parts of it that passed me by, which I suppose was all down to nerves and the occasion. It was only years later when I re-watched it, first on video and then on DVD, that I appreciated what a great game that final was. I remember the incredible noise when the two teams emerged from the tunnel. It was deafening, as Chelsea and Leeds marched out in gladiatorial fashion, led by the managers, Dave Sexton for Chelsea and Don Revie for Leeds. I quickly spotted the brilliant crimson tracksuit tops that Chelsea were wearing. My instant reaction to them was, *'I want one'*. Years later, I achieved this goal, and it still has pride of place in my wardrobe.

It was generally assumed that Leeds would be tired as their tough run-in had included a 1-0 defeat to Celtic in the first leg of the European Cup semi-final at Elland Road. They'd also been fighting for the league title, which would be won eventually by Everton. The Blues, in contrast, had virtually confirmed third place and just had a few meaningless league games to see out.

It soon became apparent that, worryingly, this was not the case, as I remember turning to my sister, Elaine, to see her anxious face and all I could think of saying was, 'This is not good.' Leeds were dominating the midfield with Billy Bremner and Johnny Giles orchestrating Leeds from there. Chelsea, on the other hand, looked nervy and jaded. It also became apparent that we were missing the injured Alan Hudson in midfield. I don't mean any disrespect to the Sponge, Tommy Baldwin, but he was being asked to play out of position in midfield following a season of niggling injuries. There was no way that he was going to break up what was the best strike partnership in the country at that time, Ossie and Hutch. And though the Sponge had a good game, running and chasing the ball down for the whole 120 minutes, we clearly missed the guile and artistry of Hudson. After 20 minutes, the inevitable happened, as Jack Charlton opened the scoring for Leeds with a soft header from a corner. The ball completely died on the beach that passed for a pitch at Wembley. I had been looking forward to seeing the Blues play on that famous bowling-green-like surface but *The Horse of the Year Show* had been held there two weeks previously and the damage inflicted by the pounding hooves had rendered the pitch almost unplayable. This didn't stop both sides from putting on a display that would put some of today's players to shame, considering the near-perfect surfaces they enjoy playing on.

So, we were 1-0 down with half-time approaching, and Leeds fully deserved their one-goal advantage going into the break. Then, out of nowhere, Nobby Houseman hit a rather hopeful shot towards the Leeds goal after Ian Hutchinson had headed the ball into his path. To be honest, it looked like the shot was more in hope than expectation but somehow Gary Sprake, the accident-prone

Leeds goalkeeper, let the ball squirm under his body into the net for the Blues' equaliser. All I remember seeing from the other end of the ground was Hutch going up for the ball with one of the Leeds players, and the ball falling straight to Nobby's feet. The Chelsea end exploded in a deafening roar and the Leeds end was suddenly very quiet. When the whistle blew for half-time a few minutes later, it came as a relief to all Chelsea supporters and the team. There is no doubt we had been outplayed and our performance had been strangely muted, but yet again we had dug in and managed to come back – and what a great time to score, just before half-time. Although Leeds had had the majority of chances in that first half, one of the best opportunities had fallen to Ossie when his shot was cleared off the line by Jack Charlton.

There was no respite in the second half as Leeds, yet again, seemed to be gaining the upper hand. Mind you, they seemed to have invented a new game call *Posts and Crossbars* as they continued to rattle the woodwork of Peter Bonetti's goal on numerous occasions. That is taking nothing away from the Cat, who kept us in the game with a string of fine saves that afternoon. There is no doubt that he was by far Chelsea's Man of the Match, though ultimately, that award would go to the Leeds winger Eddie Gray, whose ritual torture of Chelsea full-back David Webb has gone down in legend. But all of Gray's trickery added up to nothing, whereas the Cat was the main reason that we were still in the game at 1-1. Chelsea continued to ride their luck, but it ran out with just seven minutes left, when Mick Jones, the Leeds centre-forward, hit a low drive past Bonetti after Allan Clarke's header had thumped against the post (again!). All I can remember is a mass of white scarves down at the other end as Leeds celebrated what seemed to be almost certainly the winning goal. There was total silence in the Chelsea end. Once again it looked like we would be the bridesmaids – so near, yet so far, the same old story.

But with just four minutes left, Chelsea were awarded a free kick out on the left wing after Jack Charlton had pushed Ossie in the back. Surely this would be the last throw of the dice for the Blues? As Hollins swung in the arcing free kick, Hutch rose brilliantly to send a near-post header past Sprake and into the back of the net. 2-2.

For a split second, it didn't register that yet again we had fought back. The Leeds players were crushed. In fact, some of them lay prostrate on the pitch. They'd outplayed us for much of the game. They'd had one hand on the trophy and, in a season for Leeds when they had seemed unbeatable, fate had dealt a punishing blow.

A couple of minutes later, the referee, Mr Eric Jennings, blew the whistle for full time. It was the first ever drawn FA Cup Final at Wembley. All that didn't mean a toss to me. All it meant was 30 more minutes of the torture that they call extra time.

Again, Leeds dominated and rattled Bonetti's crossbar almost at will. But still Chelsea had chances, Houseman shooting just wide and a goalbound shot from John Dempsey (yes, John Dempsey) being tipped brilliantly over the bar by Sprake. There was another brilliant chance when Ossie, and then Hutch, both had shots cleared off the line. By the end of extra time I was exhausted. There is no way you can enjoy a cup final if your team are involved. There's no doubt that it was one of the most nerve-wracking experiences of my life up until then. So, honours even, it finished 2-2.

As we stood on the terrace that day watching the Chelsea and Leeds players doing a joint lap of honour around Wembley, it all seemed very strange. My God, both sets of players were laughing and joking with each other. For that brief moment in time, all the bitterness and rivalry were put to one side. That day at Wembley will surely go down as one of the most thrilling FA Cup finals of all time.

It flashed up on the score board that the replay would be held just under three weeks later, on 29 April at Old Trafford. Bloody hell! Manchester! How were we going to swing that with my mum and dad? Going to the Bridge together at that age seemed to cause them a nervous breakdown; going to Manchester would incur a state of apoplexy in them. And then, there was the problem of getting a ticket. Would there be another voucher system? Surely that would be impossible? But all of these problems were still a few weeks away.

As we left Wembley that day, my legs were still shaking. It was a very weird feeling. Years later I would get the same sort of reaction when taking speed. I think it was just the overwhelming sense of relief that we'd got away with it. But then again, as I've already mentioned, we'd had some great chances to win the game. I noticed that other Blues supporters around us seemed to be quite up and positive, but the Leeds lot looked as though their world had ended. Was it because they had been just four short minutes from lifting the cup, or was it the prospect of returning to the grim north? Who knows!

That night, we watched the highlights on *Match of the Day* on the BBC. Unbelievably, the highlights would be shown again on Sunday on ITV's *The Big Match*. Make no mistake, in those days, the cup was everything, and I mean everything. Throughout *Match of the Day* I kept crawling on my hands and knees to the screen every time there were shots of the Tunnel End, pointing out where we had been standing, to my mum and dad's frustration.

It was really strange how different the game looked when watching it on TV, rather than being there. Leeds had undoubtedly been the better team and should have won, but you had to admire Chelsea's resilience to stand up to a team as imposing and impressive as Leeds were. Many teams would have submitted to the intense pressure that the Blues suffered that day. This was highly unusual for any Chelsea side of that era, when the club had a reputation for being brilliant one week and then totally pathetic the following Saturday. This era of the mid-60s to early 70s was, in all truth, no different to what had gone before with the club. They had become a bit of a joke. The eternal bridesmaids, so many false dawns. It was starting to become a bit of a curse. I'm delighted to say that Spurs have now taken over our crown of the nearly-men, and they are quite welcome to keep it.

But that Chelsea side of 69/70 were different. Our league season had been one of our best since winning the First Division championship in 1955. Our third-place finish was a good return after a poor start to the season. Though Chelsea went on to win the European Cup Winners' Cup in 1971, that team which triumphed in Athens didn't have the grit, steel and consistency of the 1970 cup-winning side, and inconsistency would yet again rear its ugly head. In fact, no Chelsea side, until the Mourinho era began, ever played with the cold ruthlessness needed to match a team as tough and skilful as Leeds United were that day at Wembley in 1970.

One thing I noticed whilst watching the highlights was that David Webb had suffered what was tantamount to a public execution with the chasing he received from the Leeds winger Eddie Gray. I can't think of any one player in the history of FA Cup finals being put through such consistent torture. However, Webby actually saved the day in extra time when he somehow diverted Johnny Giles's goalbound shot over the bar. I've no doubt that would've been it. To come back three times on that quagmire of a pitch would have been very difficult, to say the least. You've got to give it to Webby; to keep on going in spite of the terrible coating he had received that day was a testimony to his strength of character. As we all know now, Webby would go on to have the last laugh.

When I went to bed that night, I worked out how many days there were to the replay. At the time, it all seemed so far away. But then the fear started to build. I knew that this was just a temporary stay of execution. You see, I come from a long line of worriers. In my family, this trait was endemic. I remember when I was about nine or ten years old, asking my nan if we'd be going on our annual Londoners' pilgrimage to Ramsgate, the Kent seaside town, again the following year. Knowing me, this question was most probably asked the second we got back from that year's trip. My nan replied, 'If God spares us, mate.' At that tender age I had no idea what my nan was going on about. Then there was the time when my sister and I asked my dad to work out how many days, hours and then minutes it was until our next holiday in Ramsgate. My dad duly gave us the answer after he'd worked it out, and then said, 'You two mustn't wish your life away.' Such was the culture of fatalism I grew up in. Unfortunately, this bleak outlook only seeped through into my psyche, whereas my sister, Elaine, seemed to take after my mum who, having grown up in various orphanages and also having served with the Women's Auxiliary Air Force (WAAF), was much more of a let's-seize-the-day type. I myself never seemed to be happy until I had something to worry about – school being the main cause of my concerns. I loathed it. There's a line in an early David Bowie song called 'Can't

Help Thinking About Me', that perfectly sums up my feelings:

'I remember we used to go to church on Sunday,

I'd lay awake at night, terrified of school on Monday'.

I don't think I can sum up my feelings any better than Bowie did in his brilliant perceptive words. So, in discovering a love for Chelsea Football Club, I had found my vocation – something to worry about for the rest of my life.

I went down to the fields that Sunday morning after the final, expecting to suffer a severe ribbing and accusations that we'd been lucky, blah blah blah, to not lose the final. I planned to reply calmly, 'We've still got another chance.' I would take all their barbs and remarks with dignity and good humour. When I got to the fields, the lads were already there. Chris Espley shouted out to me, 'You were bloody jammy yesterday.' I of course replied, 'Fuck off! What do you know? I was there!' So much for dignity and humour. It was OK for me to say it, but as soon as somebody else voiced an opinion, I went for their throat.

Later that summer, whilst on holiday on the Isle of Wight, my mum and dad took me and Elaine to a hotel bar on the seafront at Ventnor. It was the usual routine for Elaine and me; a bottle of Coke and a packet of crisps whilst the adults relaxed with the harder stuff. My mum and dad then got chatting to a group of people from Manchester. Everything seemed all nice and friendly. Then my dad mentioned that I supported Chelsea and how excited I had been that they'd won the cup that year. Then things turned nasty. One of the Manchester blokes said that 'Chelsea had kicked their way to victory over Leeds.' I was fuming. Then he added in his monotonous drone, 'That bloody McCreadie would've bloody kicked the referee to death if he'd been wearing white.' A red mist descended in front of my eyes. I don't know how I found the nerve, but I just blurted out, 'Why don't you fuck off!' Everything went quiet.

Suddenly the gobby Mancunian was lost for words. My dad promptly dragged me out of the bar. When we got outside, he yelled, 'I've had just about enough of you and bloody Chelsea.' I really didn't help matters by replying, 'Well, at least I support someone. You don't.' You see, my dad never actually found the courage to support any one team. His local club would've been Millwall, so I suppose when you think about it, he had a pretty good excuse. Notwithstanding, my dad loved football. He then went back into the bar to make his apologies and to get my mum and sister, while I was left alone outside, in disgrace, with only the waves breaking and the lights twinkling on the seafront that night, long ago, in Ventnor.

When we started to find out about the ticket arrangements for the Leeds replay at Old Trafford, it looked like there would be difficulties on two fronts: how to get the tickets and how to get my parents to allow me and my sister to go to the game on our own. At our age, it seemed doubtful that we'd be allowed to travel up to Manchester for a midweek game with a 7.30pm kick-off. Then, amazingly, my dad announced that one of the women he worked with in his accounts office was the sister of Victor Railton, who was the chief football correspondent for the *London Evening News*. So, obviously as they say, he knew people. My dad calmly told us all this one night when he came home from work. 'Look,' he said, 'I can get you a couple of tickets for the replay.' We were overjoyed, but our delight was tempered when he said, 'You need to ask that Dave bloke if he will take you.' Dave was a man I'd met at some of the tail-end games of the 1968/69 season. Looking back, it could have all appeared to be a little bit dodgy. When I got talking to Dave for the first time on a train from Apsley to Euston, I was just 13 years old and Dave was 27. I thought it was great that a bloke of that age was bothering to talk to me when I was no more than some snotty-nosed kid. I remember after one home game, I bumped into Dave at Euston. We'd both just missed our train and we had about an hour to kill. He suggested, 'Why don't we go and watch this film about the history of football? It's being shown in a railway carriage that's been converted into a mini cinema on one of the platforms.' Now, looking back, this all seems pretty dubious, but this was an age of innocence. I doubt today whether any straight 27-year-old bloke would ask a 13-year-old to accompany him to see a film; not unless he fancied the idea of the law battering his door down within 24 hours. I have no idea, to this day, why they were showing this film. Some strange, quirky things seemed to pop up like that in those days.

Chapter 13

The Cup at Last – Part 2

IT SEEMED that Dave was the only candidate on the list of people who might take us to the Old Trafford replay. By now, Elaine had met him, and she had backed me up that there was nothing sinister about him. But, persuading him to accompany us to Manchester would not be straightforward. To be honest, we only really saw him on the train to and from Euston. We definitely got the feeling that actually going to the game and standing with him was out of the question. In fact, we could see Dave from where we used to stand. His preferred place was the right-hand side of the Shed, with his mates. So, that was definitely a no-go area for Elaine and me.

On one of the journeys up to Euston, Dave told us that he was getting married later that year and seemed to get quite animated about the whole thing. We'd never really seen that side of him as I think he liked to portray an aura of a hard-bitten veteran of many Chelsea games, home and away. Whilst his guard was down, he told us that he was playing football the next day for his work's team. I casually asked him what they were called. Dave replied,

'Rotax All Stars.' Immediately, me and Elaine burst into uncontrollable laughter. Strangely enough, Dave didn't see it that way at all. He glared at us with a stony face. 'What's so fucking funny about that!' he spat at us. Our laughter turned into excruciating embarrassment. I have to inform you that nothing was said for the rest of the journey.

I'd also received another almighty snub in late 1969 at the home game against Stoke City. Now, on that particular Saturday, the weather was, not to put too fine a point on it, terrible. There was heavy snow falling and in those days before undersoil heating, there looked to be a pretty good chance that the game would be postponed. Did that stop me? No, it only hardened my resolve to get to the Bridge at all costs. Elaine thought I was mad and decided to sit this one out. But no, not me. I trudged the two miles to Apsley railway station in nothing short of a blizzard. There was no sign of Dave on the platform. Another quitter, I thought. And so, I pressed on with my arduous journey. When I finally got to Fulham Broadway Station and started to make my way to the Bridge, I noticed a flood of people walking in the opposite direction. What on earth were they doing? Still, I battled on to the Ovaltine entrance, only to find a sign announcing that today's match has been postponed. All of my efforts had been in vain.

As I trudged back to Fulham Broadway, I suddenly saw Dave and his mates. I bounded up to Dave expecting a warm greeting, but all he said was, 'What the fuck are you doing here?' I thought I was being really clever when I replied, 'Well, you're here.' He came back with, 'Yeah, but I stayed at my mate's flat in London last night.' Without another word, he walked on with his friends. I can still remember that moment, when that awful realisation of just how young I was, became apparent. As I stood there drenched and freezing in the sleet and snow, I felt as though I'd been given a right backhander. I could feel the crushing embarrassment and my face was quickly turning bright red. It was the utter humiliation of being shown up in front of Dave and his mates. It seemed that I was only a temporary friend, after all. It was OK when Dave was alone and we were travelling on the train up to Euston, but barring that, I was *persona non grata*. I should imagine that Dave had the piss ripped out of him by his mates, following our brief encounter. Things like, 'Who's your little friend?' I can see now that I was most probably the last person that Dave wanted to see whilst he was with his mates.

So, I slowly made my way back home, soaked and chastened. It was, all in all, a bloody miserable day and a bloody miserable journey. The next time I saw Dave on the way to Chelsea, Elaine was with me again. Dave was his usual self. Everything was fine. He was really chatty. No mention was ever made again about that toe-curling episode.

So, you can see the problem. How to ask Dave if me and my sister could tag along with him and his mates to the replay. There was no doubt in our minds that Dave and his cronies would all have tickets. As I mentioned, Victor Railton had already solved the ticket problem for Elaine and me. He had asked if we wanted tickets for the stands or tickets for the terrace at the Stretford End at Old Trafford, where all the Chelsea supporters would be massed. For us there was only one choice. It had to be the Stretford End. I'd only ever been in the posh seats a couple of times and I'd hated it. The people all around me seemed to be either overweight businessmen with very young girlfriends, or the usual smattering of celebs and, of course, there was the aroma of cigar smoke and aftershave mixed with the heady scent of Chanel No 5. To be quite honest, all of this made me feel slightly queasy. No, give me the aroma of stewed tea, foul-smelling hot dogs and the pervasive odour of fried onions any time. To me, sitting in the stands was all a bit tame and polite. The wildness and the humour of the Shed End was where I wanted to be.

At the next home game, which was the last of the season, and which ended up as a 2-1 win for the Blues over Liverpool (Ossie netting both goals), I asked Dave slyly if he had tickets for the replay and he said yes, he was going with his mates and they were travelling up on the Football Special at lunchtime on the day of the replay. I tried to find the courage to ask him if Elaine and I could come along with him, but I lost my nerve. So, in the end I did what all boys do throughout their lives; I asked my mum if she would come with me to ask Dave the burning question. I knew where Dave lived, because sometimes we would meet him coming out of his front door on the walk to the station. My mum, like all mums, said of course she would go round there with me. This was our last hope. If Dave said no, then our chance to go to Old Trafford would disappear. That had been made very clear to us by our mum and dad. Though this was a far more innocent and naïve era, it was still a bloody long way for two kids in their early teens to travel.

So, then came the day of reckoning as I accompanied my mum on that fateful journey to Dave's house. My nerves grew with every footstep. When we got to the front door, it was answered by what I should imagine was his girlfriend/fiancée. My mum had an indignant look on her face which seemed to say, 'Oh I see, they're living in sin, are they?' Hard to believe, but back in those days, that was still really frowned upon. Dave looked surprised to see me, and even more shocked to see my mum. I suppose he was thinking, *'What the bloody hell is going on?'* And was also fearing that I'd made things up about him and our unlikely friendship. My mum soon put his fears to rest when she asked him the burning question. When I think back now, there was no way that Dave could have said no. It was nothing short of emotional blackmail. Mind you, his face told a different story. He looked like he'd just won a raffle and then found out that the first prize was a season ticket for Spurs. But Dave said, 'Yes, that would be OK,' with only the slightest trace of sincerity.

However, there were provisos. We could travel with him and his mates, but we had to stand slightly away from his lot. As he told my mum, he was worried because he and his mates used a bit of very strong Anglo-Saxon language at times; it would be better if there was some distance between us. What Dave didn't know, as he'd never stood with me at the Bridge, was that I already, at that tender age, possessed a litany of swear words from A–Z. He then told me and my mum that we would have to remain in the same place on the Stretford End so that he could find us after the game. We were told we were not to move, at any cost. And then we would all travel back to London together. So, that was it. We were all set. All we had to do to bring the cup back to Stamford Bridge for the first time was to beat Leeds, probably the best team in the country.

Much has been made, in the years following the final, of the disparity between Chelsea and Leeds regarding the ethos and culture of both clubs. Chelsea were seen as the playboys of the game, full of King's Road swagger, whilst Leeds had already been christened 'Dirty Leeds'. Despite being a brilliant team, their tactics of arguing with the referee over any decision given against them and the brutal physical side to their game meant they were very much seen as being the epitome of the dour North. The press of the day would have you believe that the Chelsea players were frequenting the clubs and bars of the King's Road on a nightly basis, but in reality, this seems just like another urban myth. True, there was a hardened clique of Blues players who liked a drink, but can you really imagine the likes of Johnny Hollins and Nobby Houseman, who were comfortably married, actually propping up the bars of the various trendy haunts of the capital? I don't think so.

However, since those days, a documentary has been made about the bitter rivalry between the two clubs. In one clip, it showed Leeds preparing for a big game. They were all in a hotel with a pint of beer before them, playing bingo, with Don Revie as the caller. Then it got really strange. It showed the Leeds players being given a soapy massage, butt-naked, in the dressing room, by Mr Revie and the trainer, Les Cocker. What the bloody hell was that all about? Very strange ... Not in a million years could I imagine Ossie, Hutch or Charlie Cooke allowing the gnarled hands of Revie and Cocker probing their vitals. It was all very peculiar. I can just imagine the field day the press would have had if Ossie and co had participated in such a strange ritual. Mind you, if they had, it would most probably have taken place at somewhere like the Playboy Club, with Bunny Girls administering the soapy massage. So, that was how both sides were viewed at that time: Leeds, the dour, short-back-and-sides bingo-playing northerners, whilst Chelsea were seen as the louche dilettantes of swinging London.

All in all, that was a bit of an illusion, regarding the Blues. Whilst Leeds had players who could certainly look after themselves, such as Norman Hunter, Bremner, Giles and Jack Charlton, the Chelsea side could hardly have been called shrinking violets. Our skipper, Ron 'Chopper' Harris, was already known as the hardest player in the top flight – and then add Eddie McCreadie into the mix.

Now, whilst Eddie was a fine overlapping full-back, he was in no way above being viciously cynical when it came to the crunch. There was also John Dempsey, a real, no-nonsense centre-back, and, of course, David Webb, who resembled somebody that would usually be found in a police line-up. His craggy face looked like it had been carved out of granite. These players are often overlooked in favour of that swashbuckling trio of Osgood, Cooke and Hudson, and let's not forget Ossie's strike partner, Ian Hutchinson, who I once saw flatten that Liverpool bully-boy, Tommy Smith.

It's true that Leeds had brilliantly skilful players, especially Eddie Gray, the tricky winger. They also had Allan Clarke, who was a deadly finisher and the Bremner/Giles midfield partnership was perhaps the best in the country at that time. But in spite of all of this, Leeds were still viewed as ruthless, dead-eyed professionals whilst Chelsea were seen as the quicksilver side of the day, full of style and élan.

As the days counted down to the FA Cup Final replay, it soon became apparent that Alan Hudson would be struggling to be fit for the game. I think he even visited a clairvoyant and asked if he would be fit in time for the replay. She replied, 'I can only tell you, you won't score.' Seeing that Huddy never made the replay, I guess you can say that she was spot on.

Huddy even went as far as to visit a faith healer in his desperation to be fit for the final, but to no avail. At just 18, after a brilliant first season for the club, he would miss out on the biggest game of his life. Huddy only ever played in one other FA Cup Final in his career, and that was for Arsenal in their 1978 1-0 defeat to Ipswich at Wembley. It was a blow for him and for all Chelsea fans, especially since the injury had not been caused by any sort of nasty tackle. Instead, his ankle had given way after he had stumbled in a divot on the pitch at the Hawthorns when we lost to West Brom 3-1 in a meaningless game over the Easter of 1970.

As the replay against Leeds grew nearer, I was not only worried about the game, but the thought of travelling 200 miles up to Manchester for the match scared the life out of me. Why hadn't I just kept my mouth shut? We could've just stayed at home and watched it on TV. But no, the thought of being there to see us lift the cup for the first time was too much of a temptation. Anyway, we only had a black and white TV with a 19-inch screen and I didn't fancy that at all. We would finally get our first colour set in the summer of 1971, after I had pleaded with my mum and dad to get one. In those days colour TVs were still a rarity in the UK. In fact, when I first started going down to the fields, there was only one person who had a colour TV, and that was John Clarke. The others told me, almost awestruck, that they'd been round to see *The Big Match* one Sunday to watch the highlights of the 1970 League Cup Final between Manchester City and West Bromwich Albion. They spoke in hushed tones as to what it was like to watch a game in living colour. Of course, I was jealous beyond belief. In February 1971, I was invited by John to come around to his house to watch the highlights of the England Under-23s versus Scotland Under-23s on the BBC's *Sportsnight with Coleman* programme. I couldn't believe my eyes. I'd never seen a colour TV before. To see all of those players in beautiful, vibrant colour was wonderful.

My mum and dad resisted my pleas until the end of the season, but in that summer of 1971, I finally wore them down, especially my mum, as she convinced my dad that we should really keep up with the times and get that prized colour TV. I can still remember looking out of the front room window, waiting for the rental van to pull up outside our house with our brand-new HMV Colour Master, which came in a wooden cabinet with doors. It also had a 26-inch screen which seemed massive next to our puny 19-inch black and white set. It was, in fact, the exact same model as the one that John Clarke had, so I didn't win any points for originality.

With it being the summer, there was no football to watch on TV. In those days, when the season ended, that was it. Football ended – full stop. You had to make do with cricket, tennis, or athletics, which apart from the tennis at Wimbledon, failed to engender any interest from me. I eagerly awaited the new football season with bated breath. The first *Match of the Day* I ever watched in colour was a Watney Cup match between Halifax and Manchester United. Whatever happened to the Watney Cup? This tournament only ran for a few years before everyone lost interest. It was fantastic to see that game in glowing colour. Even better was the result. Halifax actually managed to beat Manchester United 2-1.

The first time I ever saw Chelsea play in colour was the 3-0 drubbing we received against Arsenal at Highbury on the opening day of the 1971/72 season; not the most auspicious of starts. My dad, who had vehemently opposed getting the new colour TV, was, by this time, turning his nose up at any programme that was still being shown in black and white. This was the case because, as I said, a colour TV set was not commonplace. In fact, that situation of programmes still being made in black and white carried on for a few years, until the idea of a monochrome TV was consigned to the past.

On the morning of Wednesday, 29 April 1970, my sister and I started out on our momentous journey to the

Old Trafford replay. This was it! Could we finally put to rest that 65-year-old jinx that had stopped us from being able to lift that famous old trophy? My mum and dad had reluctantly told our respective schools that we were both sick. It was a tummy bug that had laid both me and my sister low. Now when it came to my sister, Elaine, this was a rarity, i.e. a day off school. Her teachers would have instantly believed that she must really be ill, such was her reputation for being a model pupil. As for me, my teachers most probably thought, *'not again – what is it this time?'* I had already prepared myself for the fact that, upon my return to school, there was no way I could tell my mates that I had been to Old Trafford – a secret that would be really difficult to keep if we were to actually win the cup that night. But apart from my best mate at school, Brian, nobody was ever any the wiser. Such was my talent as an accomplished liar.

When Elaine and I got to the railway station, much to our relief, Dave was already there. So, he'd kept his word, thank God. To be honest, if he'd been a no-show, then I doubt whether either of us would have had the nerve to travel all that way to Manchester on our own. Dave's mates were going to meet us at Euston. Do you know, looking back, I don't think any of them said more than two words to us during the whole time we spent with them. To them we were just the embarrassment in the corner. This was our first time on a so-called Football Special train. At the time it all seemed a bit overwhelming. The majority of Chelsea fans were older than us and they all seemed really hardcore – a mixture of the Shed End and the North Stand. All the carriages were wreathed in cigarette smoke and the cracking open of beer cans was deafening. There were loads of coppers moving about the train in the passageways. They looked as though they were just waiting for somebody to step out of line. They just wanted any excuse to give someone a good kicking. In fact, a few years later, I saw two policemen laying into some poor kid beneath the steps leading up to the Shed. The beating they gave him was quite sickening. Even my mate, Steve Gallagher, who considered himself to be a streetwise London boy, was shocked. There's no doubt that in today's climate, both of those coppers would have been done for GBH.

Because we lived in the suburbs, we had to travel from Apsley Station into London, Euston to catch a train heading to the north. So, in fact, we were doubling back on ourselves. As the train sped past our home station of Apsley, which looked so sedate and peaceful, like something on a picture postcard, towards Manchester, I suddenly felt a sense of panic; a real feeling of homesickness came over me. What the hell was I doing, dragging my 13-year-old sister along with me? Looking after myself was bad enough, being only 14, but I decided it was best not to think like that. It was far too late anyway. Having said that, I could imagine the recriminations I would face if anything untoward had happened to us. It didn't bear thinking about.

All the flags and the banners of the Chelsea fans that I'd seen at Euston now seemed to have ended up on our train. The whole train was bedecked in blue and white and some people had fixed their scarves in the gaps between the top windows and the bottom windows of the carriage, to leave any person watching the train speed by with no doubt as to who was travelling on it to Manchester. Even though I was really hungry, there was no way that I was going to get out a flask of tea and the ham and tomato sandwiches my mum had prepared, not when everyone else in our carriage was necking back cans of lager. Can you imagine the scornful looks we would have received from Dave and his mates as we sipped our tea and ate our lovingly prepared sandwiches, followed by a dessert of two Kit-Kats? I think my mum had also given us some Barley Sugar sweets, which seemed to be a staple requisite if we were ever going on a long journey. I always remember my nan passing them round just before our coach used to leave the bus station to head for Ramsgate each year.

When we got to Manchester Piccadilly we still had quite a few hours to kill until the kick-off. In those days there were strict licensing laws, so Dave and his mates decided to look around the shops and then go to a café to eat up some of the time before the game, and that was the moment that it struck me just what a couple of dead-weights my sister and I were. We traipsed behind Dave and his crew like two little lost orphans out of a Dickens novel, just two poor little waifs and strays following in their wake. To be fair, Dave was actually pretty good to us in what was, for him, a pretty difficult situation. This was my first trip up to the north but because I'd been brought up in London, Manchester in no way intimidated me. In fact, next to the capital, it all seemed a bit small-time. When Dave and his cronies went into the café, I saw an opportunity to say to Dave, 'It's OK, we'll sit and wait outside and have our sandwiches.' I can't actually remember any of them saying, 'No, please join us.' It was more along the lines of 'suit yourself'.

When we stood outside Old Trafford, the enormity of the night's game sank in. There were thousands of Chelsea fans everywhere, and such was the heavy police presence, that we were kept well away from the Leeds mob. The Stretford End terrace, which would be the Chelsea end that night, was amazing and the ground seemed huge. At that time and to this day it is the largest stadium outside of Wembley in England. Of course, Hampden Park in Scotland, which at the time held 134,000 was even bigger than Wembley, but when did Scotland ever count, anyway?

It was a lovely spring evening, and the pale sun bathed Old Trafford in a warm, golden glow. Unlike Wembley and Stamford Bridge, you were right on top of the players. The previously mentioned stadiums both had dog tracks around the pitch, so you felt somewhat separated from the action. I'd been close up to the play at grounds like White Hart Lane and Highbury, but this was different. This was the cup final, and to be within touching distance of the players was an unbelievably thrilling prospect. I could just imagine Chelsea scoring the cup-winning goal down at our end – that would be absolutely brilliant. Then, sorry to say, my eternal fatalism reared its ugly head once again – what if I had to stand there and watch Leeds rattle three or four goals past Catty and then have to face the horrible sight of Leeds parading the cup right in front of us? What a horrible thought.

When the teams emerged on to the pitch, Leeds were wearing their usual all-white kit (they had worn red socks at Wembley because of the colour clash). This time it was Chelsea's turn to change their strip – and so was born the iconic blue and yellow strip that has now attained legendary status at the club.

If I thought that this game would be different to what had happened at Wembley, I and thousands of other Chelsea fans were mistaken. Right from the kick-off, Leeds tore into us. The pitch was not the quagmire that the teams had had to endure at Wembley. This time it was firm and dry and Leeds were using it to their best advantage with their slick passing. Yet again, the Blues looked nervous and hesitant. What made this even worse was that Leeds were attacking our end, so all of this played out right in front of me. When Ron Harris scythed down Eddie Gray, who had been Chelsea's main tormentor in the first game, I didn't really think anything about that challenge – just another of the hard tackles that were the norm in those days. In fact, when you watch the game on DVD, Kenneth Wolstenholme, the BBC commentator, hardly mentions the tackle, yet in today's game that challenge would certainly have been a straight red card. I should imagine that the massed ranks of Leeds supporters at the scoreboard end of Old Trafford wouldn't have even noticed it. Eddie Gray's brilliant performance at Wembley had earned him the Man of the Match award, but after Chopper's uncompromising tackle, Gray must have decided that the role of bystander would be the best option for him. Consequently, he disappeared from sight for the rest of the game. This was obviously the thinking behind the idea of switching Harris from centre-back to full-back, to take on the job of shackling Gray after the chasing he had given Webby in the first match.

The Leeds pressure was mounting and it seemed that the Blues could hardly string two passes together. On top of all of this, Mick Jones, the Leeds centre-forward, clattered into Chelsea's keeper, Bonetti, whilst challenging him for a high ball. Bonetti looked in serious trouble as he lay writhing in agony, clutching his knee. Harry Medhurst, the Chelsea physio, raced on to the pitch to attend to the fallen keeper. It didn't look good. There were no substitute goalkeepers in those days, in fact, each side could only have one player on the bench and Chelsea's substitute that night was Marvin Hinton, a centre-back. It became common knowledge after the game that if Catty had been unable to continue, it would have been none other than poor old David Webb who would have had to go in goal. But somehow Catty got back to his feet, though he was limping badly. In today's game there is no doubt that the substitute goalkeeper would have been brought on immediately.

For the rest of the game, Chelsea centre-back John Dempsey had to take all of the goal kicks as Chelsea were basically playing a cup final with a goalkeeper who could barely stand. And so, of course, inevitably just after this incident, Leeds scored. Leeds forward, Allan Clarke, evaded a couple of lunging tackles from the Blues and then slipped a ball through to his centre-forward Mick Jones, who outpaced Johnny Hollins and hit a shot past Catty into the net right in front of myself and all the Chelsea masses at the Stretford End. Although it was a fine shot and goal, having watched it countless times on TV, I'm sure that Bonetti might well have saved it had he not suffered that injury to his knee. You must remember that Bonetti was perhaps the most agile shot-stopper in the land at the time and although that strike by Jones was hard and true, there was no doubt that Catty was seriously hampered by that injured knee and lacked that cat-like spring that had earned him his nickname.

So, yet again, we were under the cosh, with Leeds bossing the game and Chelsea struggling to find any rhythm whatsoever. The only chance I remember for the Blues in that first half was when Hollins hit a shot high over the Leeds crossbar. Yet again, Ossie hadn't had a kick and our midfield was again missing the brilliant 18-year-old Alan Hudson.

When the half-time whistle blew ten minutes after Mick Jones's goal for Leeds, it was met by relief from all Chelsea supporters that night. In spite of all the Leeds pressure, they were still only one goal up. Yet again, Chelsea were hanging in there with a grim determination.

It was a great relief to see the Cat taking his place in goal for the second half, although it was obvious to see that he was still really struggling. Harry Medhurst had made some attempt to ease the Cat's pain by heavily strapping the injured knee.

Though Leeds continued to dominate, they could still not find that killer second goal that surely would have ended Chelsea's hopes of taking the cup. And as the night sky darkened, you got the feeling that perhaps Leeds would come to regret not taking those chances to finish the Blues off.

Suddenly, Leeds began to look tired as Chelsea started to find their passing rhythm, which had been missing since the start of the game. It's been well documented just how vicious the tackling was that night and present-day referee David Elleray said, after watching the game back in the late 90s, that by today's standards he would have sent at least six players off. Still, I don't believe that many people in the 62,000 crowd at Old Trafford batted an eyelid at the savage battle that was unfolding right in front of their eyes. Many old scores were settled that night. Jack Charlton of Leeds kicked Ossie up in the air. Sure, Ossie retaliated, but it stopped there. In those days you gave as good as you got. Looking back, my favourite clash was when Billy Bremner, the Leeds captain, was standing menacingly over a prostrate Peter Osgood bitching about the way Ossie had raked his studs down his shins. Whilst Bremner was in mid-flow, Hutch shoved the Leeds skipper in the back and sent him flying over Ossie's outstretched legs. I still love watching that clip to this day. Unbelievably, that brought the only booking/yellow card of the whole game, as referee Mr Eric Jennings booked Chelsea's Ian Hutchinson. But perhaps the most infamous incident of that night was Eddie McCreadie's kung fu tackle on

fellow Scot, Bremner. Though you may think that a kung
fu kick on any player is dangerous, this one was actually
aimed at Bremner's head as they both went for a bouncing
ball in the Chelsea penalty area. How Eddie Mac didn't
decapitate Bremner remains a mystery to this day. What
was also utterly unbelievable was that the referee showed
no interest in this violent assault and waved play on. In
today's game, that tackle would be an instant red card
and a certain penalty. All Bremner received in the way of
treatment was a couple of squirts of water from the magic
sponge, which, at the time, was the preferred method of
treating injured players. To Bremner's credit, there was
no screaming and shouting for a penalty by him or the
rest of the Leeds team. They just got on with it. And
Eddie Mac even deigned to give his Scotland team-mate
a pat on the head. Whether this was out of kindness and
sportsmanship, or just to check Bremner's head was still
attached to his body, remains a mystery to this day.

A pivotal moment came when the Cat tipped Leeds
full-back Terry Cooper's shot around the post. It was
yet another brilliant save from the Chelsea keeper. The
heroics of the Cat over the two games was one of the
deciding factors as to why Chelsea were still in with a
chance. But time was running out. With just 15 minutes
left, Leeds seemed to be on their way to their first ever
cup victory.

Then, with just 12 minutes left, Chelsea conjured up
a goal of exquisite beauty. Charlie Cooke and Hutch did
a switchover in midfield that allowed Cooke to advance
towards the Leeds goal. He quickly looked up and curled
a brilliant ball straight into Ossie's path. Such was the
quality of the cross, Ossie had managed to catch the Leeds
defence out on their blindside, and he sent a brilliant
diving header past the Leeds keeper David Harvey. I

was only aware that the ball had hit the back of the net when, in that split-second, I found myself tumbling down the terraces, holding on to Elaine in a surging mass of humanity. Leeds tried in vain to appeal for offside, but the referee was having none of it. And so, it was all level at 1-1.

The noise at the Stretford End was ear-shattering. All of us now believed that at long last, Leeds were there for the taking. You could visibly see their players thinking, '*What have we got to do to beat this lot?*' It was a very different Chelsea side that Leeds were facing that night. Gone was the inconsistency and vulnerability of previous Chelsea teams, and now the Blues started to dominate the game. When the whistle blew for full time, Leeds looked shattered. There was no doubt that the psychological advantage was with the Blues. For Leeds, a fear that a season where they'd been challenging for every trophy was going to end in abject failure had now become a distinct possibility.

When the teams kicked off for the first period of extra time it was noticeable that all of the noise was coming from the massed ranks of the Chelsea supporters at the Stretford End. The Leeds fans, like their team, looked jaded. The game was now much more even, with Chelsea starting to give as good as they got. Then, on the stroke of the end of the first period of extra time, Chelsea scored the goal that will be forever etched in the memory of all Chelsea supporters who watched that game at Old Trafford. Chelsea won a throw-in in the Leeds half after Jack Charlton had headed a clearance into touch. Now, where Chelsea were concerned, this was as good as a corner, such was the distance that Hutchinson could hurl the ball. He could vary his throws; one option was to the far post with a high trajectory or there was also a faster ball to the near post. This time Hutch sent the ball to the near post with pace. A group of players challenged for the beautifully accurate throw-in but, as the Leeds defenders challenged Ossie and co, the ball glanced off the Leeds centre-half Charlton's head, across the goal to the far post and straight into the path of Webb. He battled his way through a clutch of Leeds players to force the ball into the net off his cheek. It was, in all honesty, a really scruffy goal, but it was still one of the most beautiful sights I have ever seen.

On that night, from where I was standing at the Stretford End, all I could see was a great melee in the Leeds penalty area. Again, there was that split second where you weren't sure of what had happened before the explosion of joy erupted. There is always that moment of doubt when a goal goes in down at the other end of the ground, because there was no celebration down at the Leeds end. In fact, it looked more like a mausoleum.

Almost immediately the whistle blew for half-time of extra time. Now there were just 15 minutes between us and the FA Cup. It's ironic that Hutch had produced that fantastic throw that led to Webby's goal, as the Leeds hard man, Norman Hunter, had bitchily remarked to Hutch in the first game at Wembley, 'You're only in this team because of your long throw.' Poor old Norman. He who went by the nickname of Bite-Yer-Legs Hunter, had finally received the ultimate bite-back.

During the second half of extra time, as expected, Leeds pressed us back into our own penalty area. Every time we cleared the ball, it seemed to come straight back. Despite all of this pressure, Chelsea still found time to have a Hutchinson goal disallowed for offside. Again, there were mass celebrations at the Chelsea end, only to have our joy curtailed when the referee blew his whistle.

Now it was non-stop. Leeds were throwing everything at us, winning corner after corner. The minutes seemed to drag. There were times when Elaine and I could hardly bear to watch, but still the heroic Bonetti and his defence held firm. I remember that those minutes seemed like hours as Leeds threw caution to the wind and threw everything at the Blues in one last desperate effort.

The game now moved into injury time. The sounds of the Chelsea end whistling, trying to get Mr Jennings to blow the final whistle was a deafening cacophony. Some bloke behind us totally lost it as he barged us and other people around us out of the way to bellow, 'For fuck's sake! Blow the fucking thing!' For him, us and every other Blues fan, the wait for that final whistle seemed like mental cruelty.

The Blues then faced yet another Leeds attack, but this time there was no corner as the ball was headed over into the mass of Leeds fans behind Bonetti's goal. As Dempsey took the goal kick in place of the stricken keeper, the final whistle blew. There was an explosion of joy at the Stretford End. People all around were hugging complete strangers, such was the unifying spirit of the game, when all of you share that love for your team.

Now, did I hug Elaine, or anyone standing next to me? No, I did not. I found myself weeping. For the first time in my life, I was weeping with joy. I fell to my knees, crying and sobbing into my hands, trying to cover the embarrassment that any 14-year-old boy would feel at crying in front of so many people. I looked up at Elaine, and, oh God, my sobs had started her off as well. But there were no hugs between brother and sister. I think the English reserve kicked in as we both tried to hide our embarrassment at showing our feelings so publicly.

Then a strange thing happened. As I looked around, I saw that there were grown men with tears in their eyes. Men who had witnessed so many crushing disappointments in the Blues' quest to finally lift the most famous trophy in football at the time. They'd suffered so many near misses – many more than some 14-year-old kid in his first season of actually going to see the Blues in action. Of course, now I realise that that emotion of feeling choked up when your team accomplishes such an historic victory is perfectly natural. I have since felt that about the Blues on many occasions. When we won the Premier League for the first time in 50 years in 2005 at Bolton, when Frank Lampard's two goals gave us the title, and of course, when Didier Drogba scored that winning penalty in the shoot-out against Bayern Munich in the 2012 Champions League Final, the tears welled up in my eyes again. Strangely, I've never cried over a defeat. I just used to get angry. Very angry. To my shame, I used to end up throwing things – not at the games I went to, I hasten to add, but at home. After one awayday defeat, I threw our radio across the front room when I heard the result. My mum wept at the monster that she had created. My dad threatened to call the police. 'You're getting out of control, mate!' he said. Thankfully I have grown out of it.

All I can remember after the final whistle is a blur. The sight of Ron Harris going up to receive the cup was almost lost in a sea of blue and white. I can recall quite clearly, though, how beautiful the trophy looked being held aloft by the Chelsea players down at the Stretford End. For one moment I thought some of the Leeds players had gate-crashed the party, then realised that a few of the Chelsea players had swapped shirts with their opponents. Webby even donned a Chelsea bobble hat to go with the white shirt of Leeds and, of course, there was Hutch, who had initially been refused his cup winners' medal by some old fogey from the Football Association who thought he was a particularly bad loser from the defeated Leeds side. Hutch tried in vain to get his medal, but to no avail, until Brian Clough, the then Derby manager, intervened and told the old duffer that Hutch was in fact a Chelsea player and that the medal belonged to him. I know shirt-swapping was practically unheard of in club football, though it happened in international games, but it makes you wonder exactly what that gentleman from the FA had been watching for the last 120 minutes.

The reception the Blues players received from the Chelsea hordes at the Stretford End was tumultuous, but by the time they paraded the cup down at the Leeds end, they were met by a wall of silence. Unlike the modern game, fans used to stick around whether their team had won or lost the cup final in those days. There were no half-empty stadiums as the victors celebrated their triumph. Perhaps it might have been down to the fact that the police would have penned the Leeds fans inside Old Trafford for as long as possible that night, to let the victorious Blues celebrate their win. Such was the huge risk of trouble breaking out between two sets of fans who both had a notorious reputation. All in all, it must have been a living hell for the Leeds mob, watching the flash cockneys rubbing their noses in the dirt, but at that moment, all I could think, was that I'd just seen my team lift the FA Cup. It is a feeling that you never forget. And although I was ecstatic when Chelsea won the Champions League in 2012, which must surely be the club's finest achievement, nothing for me will ever top that night in Manchester when Chelsea at last brought the cup home to Stamford Bridge.

As instructed, Elaine and I stood in the exact spot where Dave had left us. When I caught my first glimpse of him there was no wild celebration. All Dave said to me and Elaine was, 'I bet you two are happy now.' Such was the level of joy he was prepared to display in front of us. In this moment of triumph, Dave remained firmly too cool for school. I was so grateful and relieved that he hadn't seen me a few minutes previously in a flood of tears. That would have been the ultimate embarrassment.

As we made our way back to Manchester Piccadilly with Dave and his mates, I felt a real sense of homesickness. All I wanted to do was to get back home – back to the beautiful south. Elaine looked as tired-out as me.

We both thought briefly about the idea of going to see the Blues parade the cup at the Bridge the next day, but that's all it was – just a thought. There was no way that I could face hanging about in London for Chelsea's triumphant return with the cup.

Anyway, I could just imagine my mum and dad's reaction to me telling them, 'By the way, we'll see you tomorrow evening. We're just off to the Bridge, again.' My parents would have been apoplectic. To be honest, I was getting a bit sick of being around adults and having to act older than my years. Dave and his mates proceeded to get stuck into their lagers on the long journey back from Manchester that night. Somebody offered me a can, which I promptly turned down. I'd previously tried some of my dad and grandad's weekend pints of John Courage and found the taste disgusting. It's strange that in just a few short years after that night, I discovered that perhaps the taste wasn't so bad after all!

Up to that point, all my knowledge of alcohol had been confined to the taste of Emva Cream sherry which Elaine and I were allowed to partake in at Christmas. It became something of a tradition in our family and we would always look forward to the pathetic, meagre amounts that were rationed out to us during the festive holiday. Of course, typically, I used to have the odd swig in passing the drinks cabinet when my mum and dad were not around. One day one of my mates and I thought we'd try the whiskey for a change. All I can remember is almost choking on the stuff and wondering what the bloody hell my dad and grandad were thinking of in drinking that foul liquid. Yet again though, after a few short years, I decided that perhaps I was wrong and soon struck up a friendship with J & B and Jack and Jim, which shows no sign of waning. In retrospect, I was right in not asking for a schooner of Emva Cream sherry that night on the train, instead of the can of lager that was offered to me.

By the time we got to Euston, Elaine and I were both dead on our feet. I was on strict instructions to phone home as soon as we arrived back in London. I later found out that my dad had been waiting up practically all night for us to phone home. In an act of kindness and relief, my mum and dad said that they would treat us to a cab back from Apsley Station. It was a job to stay awake on that train journey from Euston to our local station. We kept a close lookout at every stop to make sure that we both didn't fall asleep before reaching our destination, otherwise we might well have ended up in Bletchley. The taxi was waiting for us at Apsley. The driver instantly spotted our blue and white scarves and asked us about the game.

Do you know, I still own that blue and white scarf. It was bought for me by my dad on my first ever visit to the Bridge in 1968. I used to pin a beautifully detailed club badge to the front of it but that was sadly lost in the spring of 1971 when I was jumped by four heroic Arsenal supporters whilst walking back from our local shops. Of course, I got the worst of it but still managed a few slaps back. I remember being swung round by my scarf whilst the others lined up to punch me in the face. After they were satisfied that they had dished out enough punishment, I was left there in the street with a cut lip and a blooded nose, but somehow I'd managed to hold on to my scarf. When I got home from that beating, I realised that my prized badge was missing. Ignoring the fact that this cowardly lot could still be hanging around the shops, I went back to the scene of the crime. Thankfully, they were nowhere in sight but as hard as I tried, I never found that treasured badge and I've got to admit that even when I became an adult, I still used to glance quickly at the spot where I'd taken the beating in the spring of 71, just on the off-chance that I would find that badge. Sadly, it still remains lost to this day.

Such was the pride that you have at that age, I was relieved that there was no one home upon my return after I'd been set upon. I quickly washed all of the cuts and bruises and then proceeded to tell my mum when she came home that I'd had a ball kicked in my face during a games lesson. Such was the shame I felt in being beaten up by some cowardly Gooners. This incident was never revealed to anyone. My mum and dad never found out and if my sister reads this book, it'll be news to her as well.

When we got home from the replay at Old Trafford, my mum and dad were already up, getting ready for work. My mum quietly told me in the kitchen that my dad, who had predicted a Leeds victory all along, had tried to jump on the Chelsea bandwagon as they were parading the cup on their lap of honour. She told me that he started to clap and said to my mum, 'You've got to hand it to them, Betty,' to which my mum caustically replied, 'Johnny, you bloody hypocrite, after all you said about them having no chance.' My dad wisely decided that perhaps silence would be the best reply.

Elaine toyed with the idea of going in to school, even if she was a bit late, but finally gave in to her tiredness and took the day off. I had no such qualms and went straight to bed, where a mixture of trying to sleep in the day and adrenaline made any rest impossible. I was looking forward to watching the evening news as they were bound to have Chelsea's homecoming as part of their news bulletin. And sure enough, there they were that night, the triumphant Chelsea team parading the cup on an open top bus outside Fulham Broadway.

I couldn't believe that we, Chelsea, were the FA Cup winners of 1970. Today, of course, there would be Sky Sports News to report on every detail of that homecoming, but in those days, you lived on scraps, such as the news broadcast that night, with perhaps less than five minutes dedicated to what, at the time, seemed to me the most seismic event in my life. I couldn't wait to go down to the fields that evening to brag to all my mates. How I would savour their sullen envy. But first things first. I would have to broach the subject of getting the following day, Friday, off school as well. Elaine, of course, would be straight back to her classes but no, not me. I wanted the luxury that after tonight I would have three full days before I went back to that dreaded regime. After some well-intentioned promises that I would help my mum around the house the following day, my parents relented but my dad said, 'On no account must you go out in case you bump into a truant officer.'

You know, after all those dire warnings I received over the years during my school days, not once did I spot that dreaded bogeyman. Did he exist? Who knows? But one thing's for sure, in today's current climate, any school official trying to force some kid back to classes would have to be careful that he wasn't accused of assault. A complete sea-change from those days back in the early 70s, when all kids lived in fear of authority.

Though it was fine weather that Thursday night after Chelsea's first-ever FA Cup win, I still wore my scarf down to the fields, as if announcing to all my neighbours, any passer-by, blokes walking their dogs, that here I was, a proud Chelsea supporter, a cup winner. My God, what was I thinking of? I must've looked a right plum. But in the end, I suppose I had earned the right to be a show-off. But hang on a minute, suppose all of those innocent bystanders thought I was nothing but a despicable little glory-hunter? Like the ones you see nowadays cropping up in every high street wearing the club shirt and jumping on the bandwagon after their supposed club had secured a trophy win. Many of them would struggle to name the team from one to 11 and have only ever seen their 'beloved' heroes on the TV. No, that night I didn't want to be thought of as one of those vermin. In retrospect, perhaps I should've worn a sandwich board proclaiming, 'I actually go to the games! Honestly...'

Of course, when my mates saw me wearing my scarf, they howled with derision. Well OK, I thought, let them laugh because I would be having the last laugh and Chelsea had the cup.

One last note on that epic final; there is no truth to the rumour that after Eddie Mac's horrendous kung fu kick challenge on Billy Bremner's head, Eddie was ever employed as Bruce Lee's stunt adviser on *Enter The Dragon*. I just thought I'd clear up that urban myth.

Chapter 14

A Brugge Too Far?

WHERE TO start, about a game that has passed into Chelsea legend? Yes, there have been many great European nights at the Bridge since then: the Barcelona game in 2000; then the unforgettable night in 2005, when we again triumphed against the same opponents. But to Chelsea supporters of my generation, there is only one game that merits the title of Chelsea's greatest-ever European night, and it occurred on 24 March 1971, against Brugge.

Things did not augur well for us leading up to that game. We had lost the first leg 2-0 to Brugge and it seemed a tall order to pull that back against the talented Belgian side which included the brilliant Dutch winger, Rob Rensenbrink, who was later to become a member of the legendary Holland side at the 1974 World Cup. On the Saturday before the Brugge quarter-final second leg, I'd been to the Bridge to see Chelsea play Huddersfield. It was perhaps the worst game of football that I'd ever seen, and to this day, it is still right up there as one of the bleakest matches I have ever watched. Huddersfield, who were relegated later that season, came to the Bridge with no hope, no ambition and no clue. Amongst all of my mates who were there, it became known as the 'day of the pigeons'. It had rained heavily the night before and all of the local pigeon flock decided to go hunting for worms in our half. In fact, the pigeons crossed the halfway line more than Huddersfield did that afternoon. The only highlight of that dreadful game, which inevitably ended up being a goalless draw, was an exciting run by Eddie McCreadie, who proceeded to juggle the ball from inside our half, past the bemused Huddersfield defenders, playing his own version of keepy-uppy. He suddenly found himself deep into the opponents' penalty area, but with only the keeper to beat, Eddie fluffed his lines and dinked the ball over the bar. So, not a game to get the pulse racing. Certainly not an occasion to fill all Blues supporters with hope for the Brugge tie the following Wednesday.

Our league form had been patchy to say the least. We badly missed Ossie, who had been suspended since January for being a naughty boy. Hard to imagine a player today being banned for eight weeks just for picking up too many yellow cards. It would be a gamble to bring Ossie back against Brugge, a game that he was eligible to play in, as his ban had only expired at the beginning of the week we were to face the Belgians. Dave Sexton was a tactically astute manager for the Blues, but always erred on the side of caution. Owing to the fact that our season was petering out after the glory of the year before, when we had lifted our first ever FA Cup, there could be no doubt that Sexton would have to gamble if the club were to progress. We needed Ossie.

On the day before the game against Brugge, I decided that school was an irritation I could do without so, I planned to bunk off that morning. I got on the bus to school that day, as I always used to share part of the journey with my dad, who was on his way to work. He and his cronies always sat on the top deck at the back of the bus, all of them smoking like chimneys. My God, how the world has changed. Yes, I sat there in all innocence and played the part of the dutiful son on his way to school. My dad was unaware that when I got off at my stop and said goodbye to him and his work pals, I would just wait around for the next bus to take me home. Now you might ask yourself, why would I do that? No one was at home all day, but unbeknownst to my parents I had fashioned a special tool in my metalwork class. It was the only thing that I ever made and completed in all of my school days. This tool enabled me to push the key of the back door through the lock, where it would then drop on to the floor inside my house. I would then use my 'duplicate' key, which I had had cut in secret. I would let myself in, to ponder and worry over the events that were going to take place at the Bridge that night. What a deceitful little shit I was. My Machiavellian tendencies knew no bounds in those days. In fact, when I think about it all these years later, nothing much has changed.

In those days there was no daytime telly so, even if I decided to watch some of the shit school programmes, I always made sure that I turned the telly off at least half an hour before my dad came home for lunch, as a warm TV would have given the game away. Where did I retire to during my dad's lunch break, you may ask? Why, to the garage, of course, where I had created a spy-hole so that I could see when my dad arrived home for lunch and when he went back. Again, you might ask, why didn't I just stay away from home and hang about in the town, or get a coffee in a Wimpy Bar? Well, things were different in those days. Whilst today, you see kids out and about all the time during school hours, back then there were truant officers, and walking around in a school uniform was a definite no-no. I had arranged to meet my mate, Robbo, at the game. He didn't have the bottle to bunk off like me, so we would meet up by the tea bar at the Bridge. We planned to transfer that night on to the benches in the West Stand. I had left my hiding place in the garage that afternoon and, on impulse, decided not to wait around at home. I got an early train to Euston at about three o'clock and that left me with hours and hours to kill. I ended up on the streets of London, like a lost soul looking for the divine light that was the Bridge and Chelsea Football Club.

The atmosphere that night at the Bridge was unbelievable. It was a fact that due to the distance of the pitch from the stands, it was sometimes difficult to replicate the atmosphere you found in smaller, more compact grounds, where you could literally reach out and touch the players. Robbo and I had our usual two hamburgers before we went into the Bridge. There used to be a hot dog/hamburger stall on a side road facing the entrance to the North End of the ground. In those days, it was owned by a Scottish bloke who, although he was balding, had dyed his remaining hair jet-black. He had also managed to dye his moustache. I say, 'dye', in the loosest terms, because, to be honest, it looked more like he had used boot polish. However, his hamburgers were legendary. To this day, I have never had a hamburger so good. They were cooked to perfection, the onions weren't soggy and soft, which is so often the case with the food served outside football grounds. He also used lovely powdered, soft, white baps. We always used to eat one, and then go back for a second – they were that good.

The evening of 24 March 1971 was warm and balmy. A spring evening that seemed to herald in what was to be a long, hot summer. Surely, we would do it? We had to, we just had to. Already, Spurs had won the League Cup and Arsenal were riding high in the league and were in fact on their way to their first-ever double. There was no way that we could allow them to eclipse our achievements of the season before.

That night in the programme notes, Ron Harris urged the Bridge to get behind the team as he said, 'You were the 12th man when we beat Leeds in the cup final. We need that level of support tonight!' Not one single person in Stamford Bridge that night let him down.

And so the game kicked off and we tore into them like men possessed and finally after 22 minutes, Nobby Houseman scored following a scramble in the goalmouth. So, 1-0, but still 2-1 down on aggregate. Then a few minutes later, Ron Harris – yes ... Ron Harris! – thumped a 25-yarder against the foot of the Brugge goalpost. Surely, it was only a matter of time? Yet, at the break, we still hadn't made the vital breakthrough.

In all fairness, the game was far from one-sided. Brugge were very quick and deadly on the counter-attack and in their winger, Johnny Thio, they had the best corner kick taker I've ever seen. In fact, we wondered what was going on when the Brugge supporters behind us began chanting his name as he stepped up to take their first flag kick. That corner hit the underneath of our bar. The next one hit the inside of the far post and bounced out. I think by now, we were aware that he had no intention of crossing the ball to his team-mates. He was trying to score directly. Every subsequent corner after that brought total fear into our hearts.

Despite all of our pressure in that second half, we couldn't find a second goal. Then to our horror, Brugge almost equalised when one of their forwards took the ball round keeper John Phillips. The Bridge held its breath.

Miraculously, Johnny Boyle ran back and hacked the ball off the line. The tension was now at fever pitch. But then, with nine minutes left, Ossie finally took centre stage. Though he'd looked rusty that night, the way he moved on to Charlie Cooke's through pass and dinked the ball over the onrushing Brugge keeper was pure class. It was now 2-0 and 2-2 on aggregate – and that was the score after 90 minutes.

So we now had to endure another 30 minutes of extra time. It seemed that our second goal had knocked the stuffing out of Brugge and there was no further score in that first period of extra time. But we didn't have to wait long.

In the second half, Ossie drilled a sweet low shot from an exquisite cut-back from Alan Hudson to put us 3-0 up. The whole ground was in a state of pandemonium. With a couple of minutes to go, my mates and I started to make our way out of the benches towards the exits on the North Terrace. We all faced the charming prospect of school the following day coupled with a rollicking from our parents for getting home so late (even then, Chelsea were wrecking my life!)

We then heard the roar of anticipation as Chelsea surged forward yet again. We quickly looked back just in time to see Tommy Baldwin smash in the fourth goal. The celebrations were so deafening that no one heard the final whistle. We'd won 4-0 and 4-2 on aggregate.

And so ended one of the greatest nights in Chelsea's history. Sadly, a game that can only be recalled from memory as no footage of it exists. Now and again I have a look on YouTube, but so far, no luck.

I searched for years to find footage of the Spurs v Chelsea 1972 League Cup semi-final at White Hart Lane and unbelievably, I have now found it. Somebody has posted it on there under the title of 'Chelsea v Derby – 5/1/72'. Take no notice of this. It is in fact the Spurs game and it is brilliant to see Alan Hudson's last-minute goal that took us to Wembley. So, I will never give up hope of finding the Brugge game, because if my memory serves me right, and I do have a good memory, they did show the Chelsea goals against Brugge the following night on ITV's *Today* programme, which was hosted by Eamonn Andrews and featured a professional cockney called Monty Modlyn. Let's hope that one day some Blues fanatic will find the footage of a game that has become legendary in our history.

Chapter 15

City and Real Madrid

SO, NOW we were drawn against Manchester City in an all-English European Cup Winners' Cup semi-final – not a prospect I was looking forward to, as City had thumped us 3-0 at the Bridge in the fourth round of the FA Cup in the driving rain; a defeat made more painful as we were the holders of the cup that day.

City possessed three stars in their line-up – Colin Bell, Francis Lee and Mike Summerbee. Bell had already scored three goals against us that season – two in the cup game and a brilliant volley in the 1-1 draw in the league game at the Bridge. There was some small consolation that City had quite a few injury problems in the lead-up to the semi-final, but so did we. Ossie, who had returned in triumph against Brugge, would be missing for the first leg at the Bridge with an ankle injury.

My mate Kevin went with me to that first leg, even though he was a Watford supporter. Such was the draw of the Blues in those days. Chelsea, even though they were at home, wore the yellow and blue away strip, whilst Man City were dressed up as AC Milan in their red and black striped shirts. The game itself was a dull affair with Derek Smethurst, the South African centre-forward who replaced Ossie in the Chelsea line-up, scoring the only goal. Surprisingly, the second leg was a pretty routine away win, as Keith Weller's free kick for the Blues was palmed into his own net by City keeper Ron Healey to give Chelsea a 1-0 win and a two-leg aggregate score of 2-0. It was all a bit of an anti-climax. I think most Blues fans expected two titanic struggles but, in the end, Chelsea cruised through to the final whilst City disappeared without a fight.

So, another cup final, this time against Real Madrid in Athens. There was no way that I would be allowed to go to this game by my parents. My God, they had nervous breakdowns if I was late back from the Bridge. In fact, after the semi-final against City at home, mine and Kev's tube train broke down just outside High Street Ken, and we were stuck in that tunnel for about half an hour. It was a warm evening, so it quickly became quite claustrophobic and stuffy. The tube delay meant we missed our train home from Euston that night. Again, I arrived home to another bollocking. Again, I offered my reasons. Again, they were ignored.

We played out the remaining league games of that season but, to be truthful, there was only one thing on our minds – Athens. I remember going to a Monday night home game against Burnley. There was a pitiful crowd of just 14,000 people at the Bridge that night to see us lose 1-0 to a Burnley side already relegated. Why do I remember this game? Well, there was torrential rainfall in London that night and after I turned up early at the Bridge, I had my only ever personal contact with a Chelsea player. As I was waiting for the gates to open, full-back Paddy Mulligan walked past me and said, 'Bloody hell –

you're keen!' I just stood there frozen to the spot. I tried to say something, anything ... but words failed me.

In the weeks preceding the final there was still a doubt over Ossie being fit for Athens. There were also concerns over John Hollins, but it seemed that his chances of making the final were more hopeful. Then unbelievably, we actually risked Ossie in a benefit match for Peter Bonetti against Standard Liege, which would be unthinkable in today's game. I suppose it was a glorified fitness test for Ossie. It was a test that he failed as his ankle went again and he limped off in the second half. Around the ground, you could hear a pin drop and then, to cap a miserable evening, we lost 2-1. When I got home that night I was in a foul mood. That wasn't helped in the slightest by my dad telling me he wouldn't give me any more money for football if Chelsea kept on losing games as they needed to pull their socks up. What could I say? Nothing. I was stunned. I decided to keep quiet, discretion being the better part of valour.

Building up to the final, our local rag in Hemel Hempstead, the *Evening Echo*, seemed to have it in for Chelsea. I'd even written to them to show my disgust at their constant sniping at the Blues, aided by my dad. I raised the question, was their prejudice because we had thrashed the local team, Watford, 5-1 in the FA Cup semi-final of 1970? I never got a reply. But, the story they ran, that Sir Alf Ramsey might actually call up Ossie and Johnny Hollins for the England–Wales game that was being played on the same night we were due to play Real Madrid in Athens, incensed me. What a load of bollocks. Can you imagine Chelsea releasing two of their best players for a meaningless home international match against Wales, whilst the Blues were playing in a major European final? Add in the fact that the Thunderbird puppet named Alf Ramsey had treated the two players in question disgracefully, and it was even more far-fetched. Hollins only won one England cap in his whole career, with Sir Alf picking Spurs's Alan Mullery (unbelievably) over him for a place in England's midfield. Worse was his treatment of Ossie. Ramsey included Ossie in the squad taken to Mexico for the 1970 World Cup finals. This was when Ossie was in red-hot form after scoring 31 goals that season as the Blues lifted the FA Cup for the first time. Ramsey then, inexplicably, when it came to the crucial game against Brazil, chose Jeff Astle (yes, Jeff Astle) over Ossie. That decision came back to haunt Ramsey as Astle blew England's best chance of scoring when he fired wide of the Brazilian goal – a chance that Ossie would have buried.

There was one match report on Chelsea v Newcastle in December 1970 that I felt required yet another letter of complaint from me to that biased local newspaper. They described Keith Weller, the Chelsea winger, as taking a snap shot that went over the bar. Nothing wrong with that, you might think, but they actually printed it as Weller's 'shit shot' went over the bar. Yes, I know that it was probably a typo, but my spite knew no bounds, and I was convinced that the Watford-supporting local newspaper was obviously part of an evil conspiracy against the Blues.

It was around this time that there was a seismic shift in the history of my street team, Avenue. We'd all decided that with a new decade just beginning, we needed to update our kit from green shirts and yellow sleeves. Most of us agreed it was a bit early-1960s. The negotiations went on long into the night. So full of our own self-importance were we, that we fully expected the result of our decision to be on the *News at Ten*. Finally, they decided – I say 'they' because I stood alone – that they wanted an all-orange strip. I wanted blue to be included somewhere within that strip. I was not happy. Blackpool were the only team who wore those orange colours. The great Dutch team of 1974 was still three years away and then suddenly everybody wanted to look like Cruyff, Neeskens and co. But this was 1971. Other teams might have thought that the Avenue were a bunch of fruits but there was no way I was going to run around looking like a bloody satsuma. So, I devised a cunning plan.

I had made up my mind that there must be blue in the kit. Though I really wanted the orange shirt to be changed to blue, I thought that might be a step too far. But how about the shorts? Now if they were blue, to my eyes the kit would suddenly look brilliant. Also, it would look a bit like the Chelsea away kit of that era, the classic yellow shirts and blue shorts. Luckily, I had an ally in big Kev. Like me he was no fan of the all-orange kit and agreed to join me on a trip to our local town centre's sport shop, where we each bought a pair of royal blue shorts. 'Now what?' said Kev. I replied, 'Well, we just wear them tonight. We'll just go down the fields in them and say nothing.' Kev was a bit bemused. But that orange/royal blue combination looked great that night. Upon seeing the new blue shorts, to our relief and delight, the other lads thought they looked great and the decision was made there and then that the orange shorts were to be binned. So, I got my way, and blue definitely was the colour.

I think, looking back, that if Kev and myself had insisted on blue shorts, it would've been turned down flat by the others, but by actually modelling them that night, we swayed all the doubters over to our side. You might ask, what difference does a kit make? But like thousands of others, I've always been obsessed with football kits, especially Chelsea's, of course. I know it's a bit old-school, but I would love to see a return to the classic kits from the 1960s and early 70s. I actually hated it when collars came back in fashion on shirts. Give me the classic crew neck and long sleeves any time; elegant and timeless.

And so, on 19 May 1971, Chelsea played their second major cup final in just over a year. This time we faced Real Madrid in the European Cup Winners' Cup Final. So, all that stood before us and our second trophy in 13 months were the legendary Spanish giants. I had made some half-hearted attempt to get my dad to let me go to Athens, but he was having none of it. I think, deep down, I was relieved at his firm decision. The thought of a trip to Greece was a daunting one. I had only just met Steve Gallagher, so as yet, he was nowhere near a close friend. I would have found the prospect of travelling alone, all that way to Athens, terrifying. In those days, 15 years old meant you really were still a kid, and in most cases, boys were still happy to be boys. After all, what's wrong with being a kid? Who wants to grow up? There's nothing wrong with being young, for Christ's sake, with not a care in the world. You've got plenty of years left ahead of you to become scared of life.

So, I was resigned to listening to the match on the radio as, unbelievably by today's standards where a game of such importance would be screened live, radio was my only option. However, when I looked at the listings in the *Radio Times* that week, I was shocked to see that the Chelsea game wasn't even going to be on the radio, because the Athens final against Real Madrid coincided on that Wednesday night with the Home International match between England and Wales at Wembley, with updates of Chelsea v Real Madrid in Athens.

I made my way down to the fields at six o'clock to get an hour and a half of football in before I went back home to listen to the game. It was also a way of passing that excruciating wait for the kick-off. The build-up to any cup final is nerve-wracking, but not being able to see it was even worse. After saying goodbye to all my mates, I made my way back home. My mum and dad were watching telly, so I was left to sit alone in the kitchen listening to the transistor radio with the kitchen door firmly shut. I had decided that I wanted to remain alone in purgatory.

There I was, listening to England v Wales, not giving a toss about the result, but waiting for the crumbs that were to be sent to me from Athens. In the first half there were practically no updates at all. One report said the game was extremely tight with few chances. It was the same with the England/Wales match that I had to endure listening to. So, at half-time, at Wembley and Athens it was 0-0.

I went out into the back garden during the half-time break, pacing up and down like a nutter. It came as a relief when the second half started. Still, the bloody BBC persisted with the crap England match. Then ten minutes after half-time, the commentator at Wembley said, 'We're going straight to Athens as there has been a goal.' The terrifying wait for the news turned into jubilation as it was announced that Peter Osgood had put Chelsea 1-0 up. Strangely, I didn't really even celebrate. I just thought, '*Oh my God, there's still 35 minutes to go.*' I started looking at my watch every few seconds as the time dragged by. Still, I was forced to listen to that non-event of a game between England and Wales, which was petering out to nothing. As the minutes ticked by, there were no more updates. When I think back, it was a bloody scandal that the BBC didn't even bother to go backwards and forwards between both games. But that night, the BBC decided that Chelsea were not high on their agenda. And so, as the Wembley game entered its final minutes, still deadlocked at 0-0, I realised that the Chelsea match must now be going into injury time. Still, there was no news from Athens.

Then, the BBC commentator said, 'Well, it looks like Chelsea have won the European Cup Winners' Cup.' He'd barely finished the sentence, when he said, 'We're going straight back to Athens.' I can still remember that grainy voice from the reporter out in Greece that evening saying that Real Madrid had equalised in injury time. I think that reporter must have been some sort of sadist as he rubbed it in by saying, 'I can tell you now that the cup has been taken away from view and the blue and yellow ribbons of Chelsea have been removed from the trophy following Zoco smashing the ball into the Chelsea net!' I just sat there stunned.

I then ran into the front room to tell my mum and dad the terrible news. They offered words of consolation that meant absolutely nothing. I was devastated. I ran back to the kitchen to find that the England match had finally finished in a goalless draw. To be quite honest, I couldn't have given a shit. The BBC finally announced they were now going to Athens for live commentary of extra time. Just then, my sister came home. Both of us sat there in that kitchen through one of the worst 30 minutes of my life. Real Madrid did everything but score. Somehow, Chelsea held on and the final finished 1-1. There were no penalties in those days, so there would be a replay two days later, on the Friday night. I didn't bother eating the meal my mum had cooked me that night. I just went straight to bed. I'm not ashamed to say, I cried myself to sleep. I was convinced that we'd blown it. Yet again, there was no way I could face school, so I threw another sickie and spent the next two days moping around the house.

Incredibly, the BBC announced that they were going to show the replay live on the Friday night, which was great news, but I was still convinced that our best chance had gone. The thought of that grinning Spaniard Ignacio Zoco's last-minute equaliser was a living nightmare I couldn't get out of my head. By the time Friday came around, my spirits had risen. Perhaps we would do it, after all. Chelsea had looked dead and buried in the FA Cup Final the previous year against Leeds, but we'd come through that, hadn't we? *'Of course we can do it,'* I thought, but then you had to take into account that Real Madrid probably couldn't believe their luck at getting out of jail in the last minute.

So, on Friday 21 May 1971, I sat down to watch the replay with my mum and dad and my sister. Right from the off, Chelsea tore into Madrid. There seemed to be no hangover from the disappointment of conceding that last-minute equaliser in the first match. After 32 minutes, Chelsea won a corner and John Dempsey hit a brilliant volley into the roof of the net to give Chelsea a 1-0 lead. Almost immediately, Peter Osgood sent a brilliant low drive past the Real Madrid goalkeeper, 2-0. I jumped out of my seat and did a head-over-heels in front of the telly, screaming with joy. My dad's response to this wild behaviour was, 'Keep it down. You'll scare the dog.'

So, at half-time, the Blues were leading 2-0. Surely we'd hang on this time? But after the first game I was taking absolutely nothing for granted. In the second half, Real hardly posed a threat, but worryingly, neither did Chelsea. They seemed content to sit on their lead and see the game out. With 20 minutes to go, they took off Ossie, who'd struggled to make the final in the first place with a nagging knee injury. Within five minutes of Ossie's departure, Real scored. Sebastian Fleitas hit a low shot into Bonetti's right-hand corner. So, it was 2-1, with 15 minutes left.

Suddenly, Real looked threatening. Chelsea were relying on the counter-attack. They were defending far too deeply, but still they held on. With a few minutes left, Bonetti pulled off a brilliant save to deny Real yet another late equaliser. This time there was no late drama, and the referee blew the whistle for full time. So, we'd won the Cup Winners' Cup! And that was two major trophies in two seasons. As soon as the game was over, my mum went into the kitchen to cook my tea. Unlike the rest of the family, I had not eaten that night, and to this day, big games always affect me in that way.

We watched TV for the rest of that Friday night. What was on, I couldn't begin to tell you. My head was still reeling from the fact that we'd won another cup. How had Chelsea done it, considering the heartbreak of that first game? How had they survived that horrendous battering they'd received in extra time against Real on Wednesday night? It was revealed, years later, that after the first match, they'd all gone out and got plastered.

The manager, Dave Sexton, pulled off a master stroke by leaving the team to their own devices which was something that must have gone against the grain with Sexton, as he was teetotal and a church-goer. But somehow, in the alcoholic mist that the Blues players engulfed themselves in that night, the belief that they could beat Real Madrid took root in their consciousness. The players knew that they'd taken the best that Real Madrid could throw at them, and survived, with a mixture of skill, determination and a British Bulldog spirit.

On the Sunday, I played football with my mates down at the fields, glowing with pride that my team had won yet another trophy. Sadly, it was a feeling I was not to experience again for more than a quarter of a century.

But for now, I was able to look forward to another summer of revelling in Chelsea's glory. It was later that summer, during the six-week holiday, I went up to London for the day with my mate Kevin to visit the Football Hall of Fame. I believe it was somewhere in the West End. To be honest, and not to put it too bluntly, the Hall of Fame itself, was in a word, crap. The exhibits such as they were, were few and far between. They did, however, have some TV screens which if you pushed a button on them, you could watch various reruns of goals of past matches. I immediately latched on to Ian Hutchinson's goal against West Brom in January 1971, one of the two that he scored that day in a 4-1 win. So, all in all, it was a bit of a disappointment. They did, however, have a restaurant/café and seeing that we were starving, we thought we'd make use of it. I ordered burger and chips which they in their infinite wisdom had renamed Pele and Chips. Kevin decided on sausage and chips, which went by the catchy name of Puskas and Chips. God knows what the desserts were called – I'd hate to think. Strangely, the Football Hall of Fame lasted for just a few short months before it shut its doors forever.

Chapter 16

London Boys – Part 1

I FIRST met Steve Gallagher halfway through the 1970/71 season and for the next seven years we went together to the vast majority of home games and quite a few away trips as well. But that's only the half of it. I'd say during that time, Gallagher was my best friend, and, as we grew up, our friendship extended beyond Chelsea to holidays, going to discos, learning to play the guitar, forming a band and spending weekends either at his house in Pimlico in London or at my home in Hemel Hempstead.

I'd seen Gallagher at home games for about six months without ever talking to him. Me and my mates from Hemel thought he was hysterical. When he got into full flow on the terraces, some of the comments and insults he hurled towards the opposing teams were brilliant. Everyone in our corner of the ground knew of him and would eagerly await his next tirade. One of his best outbursts occurred in November 1970 when we lost 2-0 to Spurs at the Bridge in a fantastic match that was played in a virtual monsoon. I've never been so soaked through in all my life. To make matters worse, Spurs scored their two goals in the 91st and 92nd minutes. It was a cruel way to lose and, on the day, a draw would have been a fair result as both teams had played brilliantly on a pitch that was almost totally waterlogged. Today, the game would never have been played. Anyway, after the final whistle, as the Chelsea players trudged off disconsolately and whilst the Spurs players were milking the applause from their celebrating supporters down at the far end of the ground, Gallagher's volley of abuse summed up the feelings of all of us standing there drenched and depressed at the horrific way we'd lost the game. Gallagher pushed his way through the crowd to the front of the terraces and, with his hair plastered to his head and his programme a sodden mess in his hands, he threw down the gauntlet to Spurs, their players and supporters alike. 'Come back you cheats! You fucking cowards! We'll get you back for this, you fuckers! Just wait 'til we play you at White Hart Lane! We'll fucking murder you, you bastards!'

Unfortunately, Gallagher's promise of retribution wasn't fulfilled, as in March 1971 Spurs beat us at their place, once again with two late goals, after we'd led 1-0 for the majority of the game. Yet, what goes around, comes around. Less than a year later, we denied Spurs a place at Wembley with one of the cruellest last-minute goals ever seen at White Hart Lane. Mmm, shame.

Eventually, I got talking to Gallagher. As I recall, he asked me if I knew what the team changes were and that was it. A new friendship started in the space of a few seconds. Despite all of its critics, going to football is a great way to meet new mates. It's easy, because you have that one thing unifying you – bonding you together – the team you all support. I'm sure Gallagher's and my story has been replicated thousands of times over, at grounds all over the country.

After a season had come to a close, you tended to lose contact with the people you met at the games. However, Gallagher and I had arranged to meet at the first home game of the 1971/72 season. As it turned out, it was to be against Manchester United of all people. I told my sister about Gallagher and she wanted to meet him. Although I looked for him before the game and during it, there was no sign. To cap a miserable night, we lost 3-2 to United. This was followed by our hero, Peter Osgood being slapped on to the transfer list the following day for not trying hard enough. Thankfully, it was all patched up between Ossie and Dave Sexton and, a fortnight later, he came off the list to the immense relief of all the Chelsea supporters.

I think my sister, in a way, thought I was making Gallagher up. And so, she came to the next home game, this time against the other Manchester club, City. Again, no sign of Gallagher. I couldn't believe it, as the arrangement we had made had seemed set in stone.

The next home game was a couple of weeks away – a midweek game against West Brom. By this time, my sister must have decided that Gallagher didn't exist. So, she decided to give this game a miss. Within seconds of me taking up my place alone on the terraces, Gallagher tapped me on the shoulder. I asked him where he'd been. He told me that he'd been at those two previous home games, but he hadn't wanted to butt in 'on me and my bird!' I told him, that was no bird, that was my sister. As I was going on holiday to Spain with my family the following weekend, it was good to know that I hadn't lost my new-found friend.

Gallagher's background and home life were fascinating. I came from the bog-standard 2.4 children brigade, but he was one of 22 brothers and sisters. In fact, he told me, he hadn't met half of them. As his dad's first wife had died, Gallagher was one of the many offspring of the second marriage. He lived in Pimlico, just around the corner from Victoria Station, and the first time I went round there, I was amazed at his home life.

Gallagher lived on the top floor and I mean 'lived'. Apart from a Sunday dinner cooked by his mum, he fended for himself. Whereas I was still my mum's blue-eyed boy and had everything done for me, Gallagher washed, cooked and cleaned for himself. I think he'd had a nasty illness when he was a little kid and spent some time in a sanatorium. It was this and other events that made him so self-reliant. Everything about him was spotless; his clothes, his room, hair always well cut, clean-shaven – apart from when he experimented with a beard. To my horror, he could grow a full one at the age of 16, whilst I was still cultivating my pathetic bum-fluff.

He lived at home with his mum, two brothers, three sisters and sometimes Julian, his brother-in-law – a real character – who was, I suppose, a bit of a Del Boy. Julian was into everything. He taught Gallagher to play the guitar, giving him really useful tips as Julian had played in cover bands during the 60s – tips that put Gallagher far ahead of me in the guitar-playing stakes. Gallagher told me that Julian once got caught by the coppers for siphoning off petrol from Esso tankers. When the coppers had Julian down at the nick, they produced photographic evidence that caught him red-handed siphoning off the petrol. When they asked him if he had anything to say, Julian replied, 'I'll take this one, and I'll take that one. As for the rest, you can keep them. I don't think they capture the best side of me.' Whether the story is true, I don't know, but at the time, it became a legend.

The final character at Gallagher's house was his dad. He must've been in his mid-70s. Mind you, after fathering 22 kids, he might have been about 35. He was an amazing character. You never saw him without his cap, indoors or outdoors. He seemed to be checking the form of the gee-gees endlessly and he had this thing about people taking up space. Whenever I went round there, I was constantly told to get out of his way. One Saturday lunchtime, Gallagher and I were in the kitchen making some fried egg sandwiches to eat before we went to the match. Gallagher's dad walked in and said to him, 'You're taking up too much room – clear off!' Gallagher replied, 'What do you want me to do – stand on the fucking ceiling!'

On another occasion, we found out that the old boy was hiding his own stash of milk in the washing machine, as he was convinced other people were nicking his supply. The real classic moment though, happened on a Saturday night in 1975. Gallagher and I had been to the game that day and then out on the lash in the evening, most probably drowning our sorrows at yet another poor performance. When we got back to Gallagher's, his dad was on his own, watching *Match of the Day*. It was Man United v Leeds. We decided to join him in the front room and watch the game. One of United's goals was great. Martin Buchan hit a defence-splitting pass to Gordon Hill and his first-time centre was swept into the net by Stuart Pearson – a brilliant goal. When the game finished, they had the usual interviews and post-match analysis. Of course, they showed the Buchan to Hill to Pearson goal again, highlighting what a great move it had been. All of a sudden, Gallagher's dad shot up out of his armchair, pointing at the screen.

'Look at that! They've scored a goal just like the other one they scored earlier. I don't believe it! You saw it – it was bloody identical, it was!' Gallagher and I wondered what the hell was going on. Finally, we twigged: he'd fallen asleep just after that goal was scored, woken up during the highlights and saw the goal again. 'For fuck's sake!' Gallagher replied, 'it was a bloody replay, Dad. You've been asleep, you silly old sod.' 'No I haven't,' his dad replied. 'I've never seen anything like it – never, I tell you! There's not many teams could do that!'

'Come on,' Gallagher said to me. 'I give up!' We left his dad sitting in his chair, shaking his head, muttering, 'Never seen anything like it. What a team. What a team. Unbelievable!' And I suppose in a way he was right. It was – totally – unbelievable.

Chapter 17

London Boys – Part 2

JULIAN, STEVE'S brother-in-law, had the look of Roy Orbison about him. He had the same haircut and wore tinted glasses. Mind you, to be truthful, he looked more like Roy Orbison's fatter brother – or a hybrid of Roy Orbison and the Pillsbury Doughboy. Luckily for Julian, he had been blessed with a sharp tongue that would make you think twice about taking the piss out of him.

Only once did I break through his defences. I can't really remember the insult he'd thrown at me, but I mumbled something back under my breath. Julian then said, 'Speak up, you little fucker. Come on, spit it out. I can take it on the chin.' To which I replied, 'Which one?' Julian jumped out of his seat and shouted right in my face, 'You cheeky little fucker!'

What made it worse was that Steve was laughing his head off at his brother-in-law, and for once Julian could think of no comeback. He then beat a hasty retreat from the kitchen, making dire threats that thankfully he never carried out.

Chapter 18

A Night to Remember

IF ANYONE had told the Chelsea supporters who watched the semi-final win over Spurs in 1972 that that season's League Cup Final would be the last major final Chelsea would reach for another 22 years, I think the majority of us would have thought them stark staring mad. After all, this was our third final in three seasons. After wins over Leeds in the FA Cup and Real Madrid in the European Cup Winners' Cup, Stoke in the League Cup Final seemed to be a formality. Of course, the 2-1 defeat to the Potteries side was a bitter disappointment and it heralded a dark age at Chelsea that lasted for two decades. Despite that loss, we had the consolation of being able to look back on a win over Spurs in perhaps one of the most exciting League Cup semi-finals in the trophy's history.

The run to the semi-final had been efficient, if unspectacular. Plymouth were seen off in the second round, then Nottingham Forest were dispatched. The most exciting game before the semi-final was against Bolton Wanderers, then a third division side. I'd gone to the game at the Bridge with Gallagher, and to be quite honest, Chelsea were a bit lucky to get a 1-1 draw; Alan Hudson's equaliser with 20 minutes left, saving the day. Gallagher, Wally and a few of the others said we should all go up north to the replay. I didn't fancy it one bit, so I stayed at home and was about to watch *Steptoe and Son* when the announcer on the BBC said, 'Here are tonight's football results.' I could hardly bear to look and covered my face with my hands. I peered through them to see Bolton 0, Chelsea 6! I couldn't believe it. I was ecstatic and jumped around the front room. Then I realised what stick I was going to get from Gallagher and the rest of them. They didn't let me down. The following day, Gallagher phoned. 'We're the true supporters, you traitor! I bet you were sitting at home with your mum and dad watching *Steptoe*, no doubt ...' His insight was sometimes uncanny. I suffered this tirade for a good five minutes before Gallagher confessed that he and the rest of them had also decided against making that long trip to Burnden Park. Unfortunately, I had fallen for his little joke, hook, line and sinker. We were then drawn away to Norwich in the quarter-finals. A tough one, as Norwich at the time were at the top of the second division and in fact went on to get promotion that season. However, Chelsea's extra class got them through on the night, 1-0.

And so, to the semi-finals. It was us against Stoke, West Ham or Spurs. I just knew we'd get Tottenham. Sometimes it's not even worth listening to a draw. My worst fears were confirmed when I found out that we were to face them at the Bridge just before Christmas, with the return at White Hart Lane early in the New Year.

Winning the first leg was vital, as anything else would not be enough. Spurs, though I hate to admit it, were a really good side. They'd won the League Cup the year before and had finished third in the league, with Martin Chivers a prolific goalscorer. And with his fellow England internationals, Martin Peters and Alan Mullery, they were a formidable side. They even had the best goalkeeper – in my opinion – around at that time, namely Pat Jennings. Unbelievably they sold him to their nearest rivals, Arsenal, some years later for £40,000, which must go down as one of the worst transfer blunders of all time.

I think it was on the night of the first leg that Gallagher and I both wore our Crombies for the first time, both believing that we were going to outdo each other. I remember turning up for the game desperate to show off my new coat. I was horrified when I saw that Gallagher had bought an even flashier one than mine. His had a bloody velvet collar! And he'd even managed to sort out the red silk hankie in the top pocket, with a tie pin holding it in place! I felt like smacking him in his smug face. When he said, 'No hankie, no tie pin – *very poor*' … in that instant I felt like I was standing there in a Pac-a-mac. Though I try to deride the kids of today, looking like clones, I suppose the truth is, so did we, but with a bit more style and élan, with today's fashions turning every kid into one of the brothers from the 'hood. I feel that the fashions we wore all those years ago are still reflected today.

The basic look of 1971/72, if you wanted to fit in on the terraces, was shoulder length hair, centre parting (the crop look was dying out by the end of 1971), a plaid Ben Sherman shirt, sleeveless pullover, Levi Sta-Prest trousers, fluorescent green, red or yellow socks, Royal Brogues or loafers, topped off with either a Harrington or Crombie – and of course, the club scarf, worn at all times. This look has passed on down through the years into the Suede-head look, the Smoothies and the Casuals. Go to any game today and you can see the influences of the fashions of the seventies. Of course, in the early-season games, the whole of Stamford Bridge was awash with Fred Perrys – a look that still survives today.

And so, the first leg kicked off. Right from the start, Chelsea looked edgy, with Spurs threatening all the time. As usual in that type of situation, it was the Blues who took the lead in the 38th-minute after a terrible mix up between Pat Jennings and Mike England. Peter Osgood nipped in to put Chelsea one-up from an acute angle. And that was the score at the break – 1-0.

But somehow you just knew that Spurs would come back. Their predictable equaliser duly arrived early in the second half, when Terry Naylor slid home from short range. 1-1! And suddenly it was Tottenham pressing, with Chelsea hardly able to string two passes together. It came as no surprise when Martin Chivers put Spurs 2-1 up with a low, 20-yard drive in the 70th minute. I looked at Gallagher and he was just staring at all the Spurs supporters going mad at the north end of the ground. At times like that, you don't need words. We both knew we were really up against it.

Now, at last, Chelsea started to take the game to Spurs. With 12 minutes left, Chris Garland levelled it with a near-post header – his first goal for the club. 2-2! But more was needed. In the few remaining minutes, Chelsea bombarded the Tottenham goal. The pressure paid off with just four minutes left, when Naylor handled Alan Hudson's through-ball. Penalty! Naylor just stood there, crestfallen. After scoring Spurs's equaliser, he'd gone from hero to zero in a split second. John Hollins placed the ball on the spot. Jennings stood waiting on his line. There was a hushed silence as Hollins ran up and smashed the ball high into the roof of the net. 3-2! And that was the final score. But would it be enough to take to White Hart Lane in January? I think at the time, if I was being honest, I would've said 'no, it wouldn't'. Though that first leg had been tense and exciting, the blood and thunder of the second match made it look like a vicar's tea party.

During that Christmas period, it was the one thing on my mind. To this day, I dread the wait for a big game. The days of optimism – the hours of doubt. In fact, during the build-up to the 1997 cup final, I went through mental torture. The thought of missing out again was quickly followed on the morning of the final by thinking, *'If everything goes to plan, by five o'clock tonight, we'll be the FA Cup winners.'* That Saturday night after the win against Middlesbrough was great. To go out knowing that your team had won the cup that day is a fantastic feeling. And to top it all off, I was going on holiday to Devon on the Monday. One of the best weeks of my life. All through that holiday, I would relive the goals, relishing the fact that we'd won the cup. That win in '97 meant so much more than the victory against Leeds in 1970. One, I was only 14 back in those days when they triumphed at Old Trafford. Two, Chelsea were a successful club at that time, with cup finals, semi-finals and good league positions as the norm. Three, I'd waited 27 bloody years to see them win it again! When Chelsea went on to follow it up with another victory against Aston Villa in the 2000 FA Cup Final, little did we realise that for a club that had been to hell and back, this was now the beginning of the most successful era in the club's history.

Over the Christmas holiday in 1971, I got the flu. I can clearly remember laying on the settee on New Year's Day, tucked up under a blanket, being waited on by my mum. The weather that day was abysmal. The rain was lashing down. In fact, at ten o'clock in the morning, it

John Hollins scores Chelsea's second goal against Derby in the 2-2 draw at the Bridge in October 1969. This is the game where I was physically sick with nerves at Euston station.

Hutch scores the first of his two goals against Manchester United in the 2-1 win at the Bridge in March 1970.

Ossie goes close with a flying header against Leeds in the 1970 FA Cup Final at Wembley.

Hutch's shot is blocked by Leeds keeper Gary Sprake in the 1970 FA Cup Final at Wembley. Hutch exacted revenge later on when his headed goal earned Chelsea a 2-2 draw and the chance of a replay at Old Trafford.

Nobby Houseman's shot squirms under Gary Sprake, to score the Blues' first goal in the 2-2 draw against Leeds at Wembley in the 1970 FA Cup Final.

Mick Jones puts Leeds 2-1 up in the FA Cup Final of 1970 at Wembley. Hutch's late header was to earn the Blues a replay.

Eddie McCreadie
collapses with cramp as
the Chelsea and Leeds
players take a joint lap
of honour after the first
ever drawn FA Cup
Final at Wembley.

Peter Bonetti
performed heroics for
Chelsea in the 1970
FA Cup Final replay at
Old Trafford, despite
playing on virtually
one leg.

Ossie's iconic equaliser against Leeds in the 1970 FA Cup Final at Old Trafford. This brilliant diving header was voted 'Club Goal' of that year and defined the swagger and class of Peter Osgood, the King of Stamford Bridge.

A young Chelsea fan gate-crashes the celebrations following Ossie's equaliser against Leeds in the 1970 FA Cup Final replay at Old Trafford. Ossie remains the last player ever to have scored in every round of the FA Cup.

David Webb's winning goal in the 1970 FA Cup Final replay against Leeds. This goal, in extra time, showed the courage and never-say-die spirit of Webby after the terrible chasing he suffered from Eddie Gray in the first game at Wembley.

The victorious Chelsea players celebrate the Blues' first ever FA Cup triumph after the victory over Leeds in the 1970 final replay at Old Trafford.

A group of girls waiting for the triumphant Chelsea team to arrive at Euston Station after the epic 2-1 victory over Leeds in the FA Cup Final replay of 1970 – a picture that personifies the glamorous image of the club that still exists to this day.

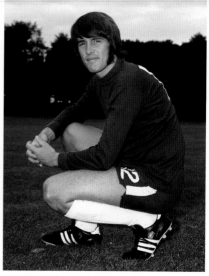

Peter (Nobby) Houseman, vastly underrated player whose goals in the victorious FA Cup run of 1970 were instrumental in the Blues lifting their first ever FA Cup. Sadly, Nobby and his wife and another couple, were killed in a car smash in March 1977. He was just 31 years old.

Ian (Hutch) Hutchinson formed one of the club's finest striking partnerships with Peter Osgood in the 1969/70 cup winning season. Sadly, injuries then wrecked Hutch's career and he was forced to retire at the age of 27. He then struggled to cope with life outside the game and died aged 54, in 2002, after a long illness.

Alan Hudson, part of the holy trinity of Osgood, Cooke and Hudson. After a stunning first season for the Blues, he never quite reached those heights again and left the club under a cloud, for Stoke City, in January 1974.

Skipper, Ron Harris, with the Cup Winners' Cup after the Blues had triumphed 2-1 over Real Madrid in a replay after conceding a late equaliser in the first game in Athens.

Ossie scores with a typical diving header in the home game against Huddersfield Town in the 2-2 draw at the Bridge on 8 January 1972.

Charlie Cooke, the mercurial Scottish winger, was another member of that holy trinity along with Ossie and Huddy – one of the greatest players to ever wear the royal blue shirt of Chelsea.

Ossie's equaliser against Stoke in the 1972 League Cup Final at Wembley. Despite being hot favourites, Chelsea went on to lose the game 2-1 – a result that heralded a dark age that blighted the club for years.

Celebrity hairdresser, Vidal Sassoon, gives Ossie a trim before the 1972 League Cup Final against Stoke.

was almost pitch black outside. Then, all of a sudden, there was a knock on the door. My dad said, 'Who the hell can that be?' and when he opened the door he found my mate Kevin Wainwright asking if I was coming out to play football. 'Oh no, Kevin,' my dad replied. 'He's got the flu.' 'OK,' Kevin said and trudged off into the torrential downpour. My dad came back in to the front room and said, 'He's got to be joking!'

About half an hour later, my old man was looking out of the window when he said, 'Quick, have a look at this.' I wearily made my way to the front room window, and there was Kevin trudging home through the torrents of rain. Apparently, he'd got no takers from the rest of my mates. He looked like a drowned rat. The weather was totally appalling. I watched as he made his way down my street and around the corner, heading for home. What possessed Kevin to make that lonely, futile journey on New Year's Day, I'll never know. But for all the years we were to remain friends, none of us ever mentioned his moment of madness. After all this time, I think what he did was great. We were all fanatical about football, but that day Kevin proved he had the edge over all of us. What went through his mind, as he set out, in a virtual monsoon, so desperate to get a game? The thing is, if I'd been well enough, I wouldn't have hesitated in joining him for a game of 'five and in'. We would have been two brave souls, kicking a ball about, on a rainy New Year's Day, a long, long time ago.

On the night of the second leg against Spurs, I still felt light-headed and weak from the bout of flu. On the train up to Euston, I felt as though I was on my way to my own execution. To have to face the game itself was bad enough – but feeling like a sack of shit, it became almost unbearable.

When I got to Euston, Gallagher was waiting for me. He handed me my prized ticket for tonight's game. As usual, because he still lived in London, Gallagher had queued up for our tickets early on a Sunday morning. He never let me forget the fact, either.

On the journey to White Hart Lane, we had our ritual of checking that we still had our tickets. Either me or Gallagher would say, 'Check tickets!' and then we would make sure that they were still where they had been five minutes earlier. What a couple of tossers!

Once we were outside the ground, we went through the ritual for the last time, before going through the turnstiles. 'Check tickets!' said Gallagher. I duly went through the motions to find my ticket safe and sound. 'Where is it?' Gallagher cried. I looked at him. 'What're you talking about?' I said. 'I've lost my bloody ticket!' he replied. Gallagher was in a total state of shock. 'You can't have!' I replied. 'I have – I bloody well have!' he shouted. I noticed his eyes were glassy, perhaps even a trace of a few tears rolling down his face. 'Give me your ticket!' he screamed. 'What do you mean?' I was incredulous. 'Give me your bloody ticket! I queued up for that! It's mine! It's not fair. Give me the fucking thing!'… 'Hang on', I shouted. 'You can't have lost it. Let's look.'

I don't know why, but at that moment, I glanced down and there was Gallagher's ticket floating in a puddle. 'There you are, you twat! It's there!' Gallagher picked it up in a flash. Though it was wet, it was far from ruined. Somehow, he must've pulled out his ticket for the tube by mistake and the ticket for the match had fluttered to the ground. I shoved him in the back. 'Ooooh – give me your ticket. It's not fair. It's not fair. I want my ball back. I'll get my mum on to you …' 'Shut the fuck-up,' Gallagher said, his honour and pride now restored. With a deep breath we made our way into White Hart Lane.

There's something special about a night game. The sound, the smells are all heightened. The sickly-sweet smell of aftershave. The aroma of hot dogs – and in those days, roasted chestnuts. Even the smell of manure and the steamy perspiration from the coppers' horses are more distinctive in the cold night air. And because of the glow of the floodlights, you find yourself standing in shadows. But in front of you is the pitch – starkly illuminated. The area, where like gladiators, the players will fight to the death!

The atmosphere that night was frightening. The ground was packed to the rafters. The noise was deafening. Gallagher and I were standing on the shelf looking down at the massed ranks of Chelsea supporters behind the Edmonton End goal. Though there were Spurs fans around us, the majority at that end of the ground were Chelsea. The wait for the game to start was excruciating, but finally the teams ran out to a cacophony of noise. Spurs in their lily-white shirts and navy blue shorts, Chelsea in their special cup-winning kit of blue shirts, blue shorts and yellow socks – the same strip that had been worn in the cup final victories over Leeds and Real Madrid. As the two teams lined up to kick off, the volume of noise increased to an ear-shattering level. It was almost a release once the game started.

As in most London derbies, the pace of the game was frenetic. Everything happening at 100 miles an hour. The tackling was fierce and ferocious. Spurs were pressing forward right from the kick-off, Chelsea playing a containing game, trying to hit them on the counter-attack. It almost paid off when the brilliantly named Paddy Mulligan (you couldn't make it up really) ran on to a through-ball, chested it down brilliantly and slipped the ball past the onrushing Pat Jennings. To our horror, the ball squeezed just wide. It was a heart-stopping moment. A goal then would've put us 4-2 up on aggregate.

Chelsea were made to pay dearly for that miss when, a minute before half-time, disaster stuck. The ball was partly cleared to the edge of the box. Unfortunately, it fell straight to the feet of Martin Chivers. He hit his shot, hard and low into the bottom right hand corner of Bonetti's goal. 1-0 down! They barely had time to kick off before the whistle blew for half-time. It was a sickening blow. Spurs ran off to tremendous applause, whilst the Chelsea end was deafeningly silent. It was not looking good. Apart from Mulligan's half-chance, Chelsea had been battered. They desperately needed some of their big-name players to start living up to their star billing.

The second half got under way, and already you could see the change. Spurs looked like they were sitting back on their lead, trying to commit Chelsea. Charlie Cooke in particular was taking over the midfield. With Alan Hudson and John Hollins in tandem, they started to rip Spurs apart. With 18 minutes left, Cooke slipped the ball into Chris Garland's path, he ran with the ball, cut across two Spurs defenders and hit a hurtling 20-yard drive past Jennings. As the ball hit the net, the Chelsea supporters behind the Spurs goal went berserk. Gallagher and I were jumping up and down, hugging each other. 1-1, and Chelsea ahead on aggregate.

Unbelievably, the game swung again. Now it was Spurs's turn to pin Chelsea back. We were defending too deep. 'Get out! Get out! For fuck's sake!' was the common scream from the Chelsea end. But no matter how hard they tried, Chelsea were reeling. I started looking at my watch: 15 minutes to go … ten minutes to go … surely, we would hang on? Then, with eight minutes left, Chivers lined up one of his long throw-ins. He hurled the ball high into the Chelsea penalty area. A clutch of players went up for it and there, frozen in the floodlights, was Alan Hudson, inexplicably punching the ball away. Penalty! Hudson dropped to his knees. Gallagher and I just stood there, totally numb. I couldn't believe it. Eight minutes left. Eight minutes to Wembley.

Martin Peters put the ball on the spot, ran up and sent Bonetti the wrong way. 2-1! And the tie was level again. At that moment I didn't know if I could face extra time. It might sound stupid, but I felt like running out of the ground. To face another 30 minutes of this torture would be unbearable. With five minutes left, Spurs broke through again. But somehow Bonetti brilliantly tipped away Chivers's goalbound shot. Spurs knew they had us now and they were being roared on by the home fans. The whole place was in a state of pandemonium. With the referee looking at his watch, Chelsea were awarded a free kick, right by the corner flag. In all fairness, it looked like a dubious decision as Mike England nudged Peter Osgood in the back. Seeing as they'd been kicking lumps out of each other all night, I suppose the referee decided it was Ossie's turn to get the decision.

In one last act of desperation, Chelsea sent all the big men up: Webb, Dempsey, Osgood ... all waiting for one last chance. Hudson looked up, took the free kick and sent in a low scuffed drive to the near post. It looked a total waste. The ball went straight to Spurs's full-back, Cyril Knowles, who was guarding the near post. He tried to hack it clear, but somehow the ball went under his boot. Jennings was clearly unsighted as the ball trickled through his legs, ran along the goal line, hit the far post and rolled gently, oh so gently, into the net.

For a split second there was silence. And then the Chelsea end exploded! It was a goal! A horrible, cruel, scrappy goal! But Chelsea were level, 2-2 and ahead 5-4 on aggregate. Me and Gallagher were going mad. A girl behind me jumped on my back. At times like that, you find yourself hugging complete strangers. It really is a moment of madness. The Spurs supporters around us were ashen-faced as they were jostled around by the delirious Chelsea fans.

Spurs restarted the game. But as they kicked off, the referee blew the final whistle. The scenes amongst the Chelsea players and supporters were amazing. The players ran to our end, fists clenched as they celebrated. A few of the Spurs team were lying on the pitch; a few of them were on their knees. They were devastated. I couldn't believe it. Chelsea were at Wembley and we'd finally got Spurs back for the 1967 FA Cup Final defeat.

As we made our way out of the ground, I looked at my hands and they were shaking. Football can be a brilliant game. It's also one of the cruellest. But at that moment, I couldn't have given a flying fuck for Tottenham and their miserable supporters. We'd done them!

The Seven Sisters Road, that night, was a pretty scary place to be, with running fights breaking out all the way back to the tube station. We quickly took off our scarves and hid them under our Crombies. To our way of thinking, there was only one type of hero – and that was a dead one.

The train back to Euston was packed with Chelsea fans. In that confined space, the noise of the songs and chants was ear-splitting, but brilliant. I said goodbye to Gallagher at Euston as he was going on to Victoria. It had been an incredible night. To this day it still ranks as one of the greatest games I've ever seen – a victory that tasted even sweeter as we had denied our arch enemy, Spurs, a place at Wembley. I suddenly remembered my mate, John Clarke, a Spurs supporter, who had been to the game that night. Instantly, I thought, *'pay-back time'*. I'd been with him to the two Spurs v Chelsea games the season before and Chelsea had lost both times. I made my way up the platform at Euston looking in all of the carriages. Finally, I saw John, sitting on his own. He hadn't seen me. In that instant, I knew I couldn't take the piss out of him. His hair was dishevelled. It looked like he'd been trying to pull it out by the roots. And his eyes looked red and swollen from crying. I got into the carriage and sat opposite him – and I've got to say that he was more noble and sporting than I would have been if the result had gone the other way. Since that night, I've learned not to rub it in to a mate who supports the team you've just beaten, because in football, what goes around, comes around.

I ran home from the station that night to watch the highlights on TV. A fantastic way to end a fantastic night. It's history now, that Chelsea lost the final to Stoke and entered into an abyss that lasted for over 20 years. But that night in January 1972 belonged to Chelsea and their fans. For that night, at least, we were Kings of London!

Chapter 19

The Gathering Storm

THERE IS no doubt that the decline of the Chelsea team that had won the FA Cup in 1970 and the European Cup Winners' Cup in 1971 started in the last week of February and the first week of March, 1972. We were never as consistent as that cup-winning side of 1970 which, to this day, still remains one of the finest teams that Chelsea have ever produced. But we were still one of the best sides in our country, and, on our day, could beat anyone.

On Saturday, 26 February 1972, I went over to the fields to play football with my mates, as I couldn't get a ticket for our fifth-round FA Cup tie at Orient. But I ask you, Orient! Who were they? Some piddling little team, languishing in the Second Division's relegation places. We decided that day to use the school's playground for our game, adjacent to the fields where we used to play football. The caretaker was a right royal pain in the arse and used to chase us off on a regular basis. I remember one night, he came running down the fields, shouting and screaming. We all ran for it. I got a bit cocky and threw a lump of mud at him. Unbelievably, from quite a distance,

I hit him smack, on his forehead. He charged after us like a mad bull. But he was a middle-aged bloke and we were teenagers, so not surprisingly, he didn't catch us. During that game on the school playground, one of my mates was late coming down to play, and so he had the latest scores. Chelsea are two up, he told us. Brilliant. We were looking certs for the quarter-finals, and that would set us up for next Saturday, when we were at Wembley for the League Cup Final against Stoke, where we were odds-on favourites to take the trophy.

I got home at about 4.30 and I was shocked when my dad said that it was now 2-2. I couldn't believe it. I went to the kitchen to put on the radio. It wasn't the featured game but there were updates coming through all the time. Suddenly, they announced that there had been another goal at Brisbane Road. Surely, we had taken the lead again, but to my horror, the reporter was saying that Fairbrother had put Orient ahead 3-2, with only a few minutes left – and that was the final score.

How had it happened? Losing to a team like that. And to make matters worse, we had another power cut that night, which was all down to the miners' strike. So, sitting there in the dark only heightened the disappointment. I phoned my mate, Gallagher, who had actually gone to the game. He said some Chelsea fans had run on to the pitch to try to get the game called off. I've never heard him sound so miserable. I asked if he was still coming down to my place for the weekend, ready to travel to the League Cup Final. He mumbled, 'I don't know, perhaps …' There was a horrible, creeping realisation on my part that next Saturday was it. Mess that up and we would end the season without a trophy, for the first time in three years. But surely not? I mean, after all, it was only Stoke. But then again, it had only been Orient, hadn't it.

Unfortunately, the power came on again at ten o'clock that evening, just in time to watch *Match of the Day*, which, of course, featured Orient versus Chelsea as its main game. Knowing the result, I looked on in horror as Chelsea, playing in the yellow and blue away strip, took a two-goal lead with goals from Ossie and Webby. It looked like we were coasting, a mere formality. Perhaps that was the problem. On the stroke of half-time, Phil Hoadley pulled one back for Orient. I doubt if he had ever hit the ball so sweetly before or after. The ball flew into the net from about 30 yards. So, at half-time, we went in, still leading 2-1.

At the start of the second half there was a terrible mix-up in our defence with Webby pushing the ball past Bonetti, straight into the path of the oncoming Micky Bullock, to equalise. Again, we had chances to win it comfortably but with the final whistle approaching, Orient's Barry Fairbrother ran on to a pass and beat Bonetti with a low shot to put Orient 3-2 up. We still had one more chance to save the game but Webby blasted over from close range when it would have been easier to score. And that was it. Out. Little did we know that in that moment, this result would start a chain of events that would lead the club into a new dark age.

On the Sunday after the Orient game, our street team, Avenue, played our bitterest rivals on their pitch. I scored a hat-trick that day, including a diving header that was similar to Ossie's goal in the cup final against Leeds. I then completed the hat-trick with a 30-yard shot into the top corner. They were two of the best goals I ever scored for Avenue.

The game itself was pretty fierce with tackles flying all around. Now, in those games, you must remember that there was no referee, so all the rules had a tendency to fly out of the window. One little shit was really putting himself about and caught me a couple of times with some nasty, over-the-top tackles. Like a fool, I just took it and got on with the game. A couple of years ago, whilst visiting my mum and dad, I saw the said little shit walking down the road. Do you know I actually stopped the car and contemplated giving him a slap. The red mist was descending, but luckily common sense prevailed and got the better of me and I reluctantly drove on. But, oh how sweet it would have been to have given him a back-hander. But then again, if I'd got nicked, I don't suppose my defence of the fact that I was only getting him back for a game that was played over 40 years ago would have held much water.

So, after the disappointment of the Orient result the game before, that game with Avenue was a great lift to me, personally. Of course we would beat Stoke. Hadn't we overcome Leeds in the FA Cup Final of 1970 when they were one of the best sides in Europe? We had also overcome Real Madrid the following year in the Cup Winners' Cup Final. Not the best Real Madrid side ever, but still a huge name in world football. During the following week, before the trip to Wembley, I tried to make a banner with the help of my sister, but we both gave up when we came to the conclusion that it looked total crap.

Gallagher was coming down on the Friday night before Wembley so that we could travel up together for the final. I must admit that I was starting to have nagging doubts about the final. That Orient result had cast a shadow over the game. I had promised Gallagher that he would get a game on the Sunday with Avenue, as we were a couple short for the replay against the team that we had drawn against the previous Sunday. Surely things would go well this weekend? Chelsea would win the League Cup and I would add a couple of goals to the hat-trick I had scored last week.

Gallagher came down on the Friday night. I used to go and meet him from the local station, and let me tell you, it was a long walk back to my home. Strangely, Gallagher seemed to have something on his mind. He looked distracted. Was it nerves over Wembley? He then blurted it out. 'You know all your mates call you Neilsyboy?' 'Yeah, so what?' I replied. 'Well,' he said, 'I think Steve is a bit boring and I would like to be known as Roxy from now on.' I laughed so hard I almost fell over. It was the type of laugh where your stomach hurts. I had to hold on to the railings of the fence we were walking past. He just stood there with a murderous glare on his face. 'What's your fucking problem, you twat?' he shouted at me. When I got my breath back, I said, 'Other people have to give you a nickname, not yourself, you plum.' We walked the rest of the way in a totally embarrassed silence. It was never, ever, mentioned again.

On the morning of the final, we both got dressed in our match outfits, i.e. Crombies, Ben Sherman button-down shirts, tonic trousers and of course, the obligatory Doc Martens. When I went upstairs to Gallagher's room to see if he was ready, I found him giving his Doc Martens another going over. I said, 'Come on, Gallagher. We're going to be late.' 'One more polish before Wembley,' he cried. I replied, 'If you're going to do that, at least use the toilet.' It was a phrase that he was never allowed to forget.

When we arrived at Wembley Central, it was packed with Chelsea fans. We made our way, with the blue and white hordes, up Wembley Way. I don't remember seeing much of Stoke, but perhaps that's just my memory painting a rosy picture of that day's events. The noise itself was tremendous. Chelsea had been allocated the Tunnel End. The same end that we had had against Leeds in 1970. You could see Stoke down at the far end of the ground. Their noise couldn't match ours. Surely, we would beat this lot? The Tunnel End was a mass of banners. There was blue, white and yellow everywhere. We were to wear our lucky cup-winning strip that day. Blue shirts, blue shorts with a yellow stripe, and yellow socks. Surely this omen would carry us through?

There was a competition organised by *On the Ball* – ITV's Saturday football show. It was a penalty competition for kids run by Mr Chinny himself, Jimmy Hill. To be quite honest, I was not interested in any way, shape or form. I just wanted the game to kick off. The waiting was terrible. Then we saw the Chelsea players inspect the pitch, all in their cup final suits. Amongst the players, I saw Hutch. What a crying shame that he was still out injured. His bravery and strength had never been replaced in our forward line. There was no greater thrill in those days than seeing your team walk out at Wembley. The gladiatorial entrance from the Tunnel End was something magical. The new Wembley has none of the grandeur of the old stadium. To me, the arch looks like a rather sad afterthought. Nothing will ever compare to the sight of the twin towers in all their glory.

Chelsea certainly looked the part that day, with yellow and blue tracksuit tops. Stoke, by contrast, looked like they'd got their tracksuit tops from the equivalent of today's Poundland. I don't know if it was overconfidence, but when we kicked off, John Hollins tried to score from the halfway line. I thought for years that that was just my memory playing tricks with me. But no, there it is on YouTube. To try and score from there, against Gordon Banks, who at the time was considered to be the best goalkeeper in the world, was pushing it a bit, and it also gave Stoke an early touch of the ball.

Worse was to follow. In the fourth minute, Peter Dobing took a long throw for Stoke. It caused panic in our box. The ball seemed to deflect off John Dempsey. Bonetti had come off his line but found himself stranded in no man's land, allowing Terry Conroy to head into an empty net. The worst possible start, and it happened right in front of us all at the Tunnel End.

After that shock, we settled down and seemed to be getting on top. But the game-changing moment came in the 38th minute. Paddy Mulligan twisted his ankle on the Wembley turf (he had been brilliant in both games against Spurs as a marauding left-back). Chelsea immediately brought on Tommy 'the Sponge' Baldwin, who was a forward, so Nobby Houseman, the best crosser of the ball in the team, had to fill in at full-back. It unbalanced the team somewhat, which became more apparent as the game went on.

On the stroke of half-time, Chelsea equalised. Charlie Cooke crossed into the box, Webby went for it and caused confusion in the Stoke defence. The ball fell to Ossie, whose first shot was blocked. However, as he fell, he managed to scoop the ball past Banks and into the net. The whole of the Tunnel End exploded. Surely, this was a devastating blow to Stoke? The worst time to concede a goal. Almost immediately, the whistle blew for half-time. Now we had the match in our hands.

We had dominated the game, more or less, and we also had the bonus of Chelsea attacking our end in the second half. Again, we bossed the game but there was a nagging doubt growing that we needed to turn this domination into a goal. Stoke still looked dangerous on the break, but there still seemed to be a feeling between Chelsea players and supporters that it was only a matter of time before we took the lead. And then with 17 minutes left, Terry Conroy of Stoke skinned Webby out on the wing before crossing the ball to the far post, where John Ritchie headed the ball down for Jimmy Greenhoff to blast it towards Bonetti's goal. Somehow the Cat managed to parry the shot, but the loose ball fell to George Eastham, the 37-year-old, to score for Stoke. It was a goal straight out of the pages of *Roy of the Rovers*, as Eastham had only come back to play for Stoke after coming out of semi-retirement in South Africa.

There was only 15 minutes left in which to equalise. We laid siege to the Stoke goal, but again and again we were denied by Banks, who was having one of those games. Stoke nearly added a third, when Ritchie's header was cleared off the line by Houseman. In the last few minutes, Chelsea's Chris Garland was put through with only Banks to beat. We waited for the net to bulge, but Banks brilliantly smothered the shot and that was it.

I can only say that seeing your team lose a cup final at Wembley is a totally miserable experience. To see the other end of the ground celebrating is horrible. In those days, the losing team's supporters tended to stick around after the final whistle, unlike today's supporters, who seem to go home so that they don't have to watch their opponents receive the trophy. Personally, why Gallagher and myself stayed to watch this, I will never know. Some kind of morbid fascination, I suppose.

On the way out of Wembley, some silly old sod of a Stoke supporter approached us and said, 'Cheer up lads, we've waited 104 years for this.' Gallagher replied, 'Let's hope it's another 104 years before you win something again, you stupid old tosser!' What a plum that old boy was. He could just as easily have got his head caved in by some of our lot and he would have totally deserved it.

The train home was full of Chelsea and it was like a morgue. At one of the stations on the journey back, a couple of Arsenal fans got on. One of them started singing, 'Come on Stoke'. He was immediately punched in the face by some Chelsea supporters. For some obscure reason, he looked shocked, but at least that shut him up.

That Saturday evening, Gallagher and I stayed in and watched TV at my place. Gallagher suggested that we should have a game of Subbuteo. I was much better than him at this game, so he let me be Chelsea and he was Stoke. I subsequently beat him 17-0. But alas it was no comfort to either of us.

I've looked back at that game against Stoke on YouTube. They've now got the whole 90 minutes on there. I thought perhaps, at 16 years of age, I might have misread that match, you know, the syndrome of looking at things through blue and white goggles. But no, we did dominate the game and played much better than we had in the 1970 final against Leeds at Wembley. But similarly to us winning the Champions League in 2012, nothing was going to stop Stoke from winning the League Cup that year. Their name was written on it. And Eastham, the scorer of their winning goal, still holds the record of being the oldest player ever to score in a Wembley cup final.

And now, the bright sunshine that had shone over us for two years, was disappearing into a black cloud. The following day, it pissed down with rain from morning to night. Steve and I played in our game with the Avenue against the other street team. Where we had been unlucky the previous week just to come away with a draw, this week, on a waterlogged pitch, we got absolutely hammered. After the way that week had gone, what did I expect? And so, ended a truly miserable weekend. Little did we know that this was just a harbinger of what was to come.

Chapter 20

That Hell-Bound Train

BY THE time we played Birmingham away in September 1972, Steve Gallagher and I had been to about three away games that season. They'd all passed off pretty smoothly, apart from me getting half pissed at Coventry, having my face slapped by a copper when all I wanted to do was go across the road to the garage to use the toilet. For some reason, the copper decided to take his spite out against all 'cockneys' by belting me round the head as I stepped out of the line of Chelsea fans being led to Highfield Road.

Later on that afternoon, as Chelsea went into a 3-1 lead, I started laughing at Coventry's vain efforts to get into the game. I was told by the home fans standing near me, 'If you don't shut your mouth, we'll hang you from the fucking floodlights!' Strangely enough, I took their advice, deciding that as we were going to win the game, discretion was the better part of valour.

On the Saturday morning of the Birmingham match, we all met up at Euston with no idea of the horrors to face us. It was our ritual then to buy our four cans of McEwan's Tartan Bitter each, for the journey. I must explain that

McEwan's Tartan Bitter was such a load of watered-down piss, it made Watney's Party Seven seem like Carlsberg Special Brew. For this game, Gallagher and I were joined by his mate Kevin, who'd never been to an away game before. He was a bit nervous, as the 'football special' trains as they were called in those days, were notorious to say the least. 'Nothing to worry about,' we assured him – both of us veterans of at least three away trips! So, we made our way up the platform to find a nice quiet compartment for the journey. British Rail generally used the shittiest, most ancient and decrepit trains they could find for these trips. Imagine the final scene from *Brief Encounter* and you'll get the idea. You know, every time one of those trains pulled out of the station, I half expected to see Celia Johnson waving us off with a hanky in her hand and silent tears rolling down her face.

We eventually settled in our compartment. Nice and quiet, well away from the rest of the nutters further down the train. We quickly made ourselves comfortable – then the three of us cracked open our cans of McEwan's and settled back for a nice, relaxing, peaceful journey. All of us 16 years old, going on 35. It was then that our world collapsed.

Five mad men – and that's the only way I can describe them – crashed into our compartment. They were all building workers, still wearing their donkey jackets and a few of them still had their hard hats on. One of them looked a particularly nasty case as, incredibly, he was still in his pyjamas. They were all, to a man, horribly pissed. It was eleven o'clock in the morning. The noise they made was deafening. They were screaming at the top of their lungs, 'We're the only whites in Notting Hill Gate – Doo-da, Doo-da!' It almost seemed like their war cry! The three of us were absolutely terrified. We sat there mute and as still as statues. Finally, the train pulled away and there we were, trapped in the middle of *Dante's Inferno*. I don't think they actually took any notice of us. They were too busy creating total mayhem.

All of these blokes were in their mid-20s. When you're 16, that seems ancient. They then proceeded to start hurling empty cans and anything else in reach through the small top window in our compartment. I was facing Gallagher. He was staring back at me with a look of absolute terror on his face. Suddenly, one of these lobbed cans rebounded against the window and cracked Gallagher on the head. Do you know, his expression never changed as the can ricocheted off his nut on to the floor. Gallagher still carried on staring at me with the same look of bug-eyed terror.

Our uninvited guests then started fighting amongst themselves. At one time, two of them fell across my lap. Still, I sat there, motionless. They then fell on to the floor, grabbed another one of their cohorts and proceeded to rip his underpants clean off by ripping them upwards from the waistband. God knows how it didn't split him in two. They then decided to throw his pants through the window.

Kevin, this being his first trip, spent the whole two-hour journey looking like he was going to faint. The mad man in his pyjamas, frighteningly, sat down next to me and told me how great Man United were – his breath almost knocking me backwards. The smell of it was enough to get you half pissed. It turned out that they were all 'Cockney Reds', hitching a ride on the Chelsea train so they could get to United's match at nearby West Brom. I totally brown-nosed it and went along with everything he said. 'Yeah yeah, George Best ... yeah yeah, Denis Law ... yeah yeah, Bobby Charlton ... European Cup Final

1968 ...' I then noticed he had tobacco stuffed in one of his ears! Don't ask!

When we finally pulled into Birmingham New Street, I'd never felt so relieved in my life. As suddenly as they had descended on us, they left. They were jumping out of the train as it was slowing down coming into the station, and the last I ever saw of them was 'pyjama-man' being frogmarched down the road by two coppers. It was then that I noticed he really did only have his pyjamas on, as it was quite clear to see that his old todger was flapping around in the breeze as he was led away, presumably to a Black Maria to join the rest of his motley crew.

The game that day seemed to take a back seat to the events leading up to it. As far as I can remember, Birmingham led 1-0 at half-time; usual Chelsea, overrun and looking as though they couldn't give a toss. In the second half it was a different story altogether. Osgood equalised and then David Webb put us 2-1 up, only for Birmingham to snatch a draw ten minutes from time through Bob Latchford.

My strongest memory of that game is Chelsea's away strip that day: red shirts, white shorts, green socks. I think our manager, Dave Sexton, was a big fan of the great Hungarian team of the 50s who wore that same strip. Talking of kits, I've never known a team like Chelsea for getting so ponced up. From the classic 1970s away strip – yellow shirts, blue shorts – to the blue-black striped Inter Milan shirts worn only once in the disastrous 2-0 defeat to Sheffield Wednesday in the 1966 FA Cup semi-final, and finally the grey/orange monstrosity of the mid-90s. I don't think there's ever been a team like Chelsea for experimenting with some of the weirdest and most colourful concoctions ever seen on a football field.

The atmosphere at the game that day was ugly and hostile, and you could sense it was all brewing up for some nasty trouble. After the match had finished, as we made our way back down to the station, Gallagher, Kevin and I went into the newsagents to buy some sweets for the journey but then decided we also wanted chips. As we came out of the chip shop, some pillock in a car was trying to force his way through the crowd. As he edged forward, he rolled down his window to let loose a stream of obscenities at the Chelsea supporters in his way. A bad move on his part on two counts. They were the hardcore firm he was picking on and he was driving a poxy little mini. In the blink of an eye, they dragged him out of the car, gave him a right slap and turned his car on its side. We didn't have much time to take all of this in as suddenly we heard the thunderous noise of stampeding feet heading in our direction. It was 'Birmingham' and they were after our blood. Not to put too fine a point on it, we bloody well ran for it. There were hundreds of them. Some poor sod in front of me, in his desperation to get away, fell over his own feet in the panic. He actually asked me for help. I responded by jumping over him! I was vaguely aware of Gallagher and Kevin – but I'm afraid it was every man for himself. We were hopelessly outnumbered. On and on we ran through the winding streets of Birmingham until finally we could see the entrance to Birmingham New Street Station. The coppers were screaming at us to get a bloody move on. As we hurtled through the station gates, the police slammed them shut straight in the faces of the Birmingham mob. They hit it like an express train, still trying to kick and punch us through the gates.

I've often wondered about the venom and desperation on their faces that day. I truly believe if they'd have got hold of us, they'd have ripped us apart. Down the years, there's been a strong belief about the north-south divide, due to those living beyond the Watford Gap having an inferiority complex, believing they have it harder up there than we do down in the south – 'Never trust the flash cockney.' On our part, we thought of them as knuckle-scraping Neanderthals. Harsh perhaps, but then again – have you ever been to Birmingham!

None of us could wait to get on the train back to London. It was packed to bursting. Finally, we pulled out of Birmingham New Street. Good riddance was the general feeling. There must've been at least eight of us crammed into our compartment, and all seemed to be going well when all of a sudden the train stopped. We waited for about 20 minutes, then eventually we were on our way again. Worryingly, we seemed to be crawling along. After about an hour we arrived in Wolverhampton. Something was definitely wrong. Gallagher got up and asked a copper what was going on. The copper told Gallagher that some Birmingham supporters had tried to derail the train by throwing iron bars across the rails. Charming! He told us we'd be going back into Birmingham New Street to pick up a few more stragglers who'd been left behind. As the train was already packed, we thought this was total madness.

As the train moved back into Birmingham New Street, we could see the platform was full of Man United fans waiting for the train back up north. There was instantly loads of catcalls and abuse flying between both sets of supporters. Loads of Chelsea were hanging out of the windows winding up the Man U fans as we passed through the station at a snail's pace. One of their lot got too close to the train, giving it plenty, when all of a sudden, a couple of Chelsea lads managed to grab his scarf and hoist him up off his feet against the door of the train. Three or four of them held him there whilst we were still moving and took turns in using his face as a punchbag. They then proceeded to throw him back on to the platform where he landed bone-jarringly, right on his arse. Looking back, I suppose it was all pretty horrible stuff, but at the time when you're caught up in it, well I've got to admit, it was brilliant. It was a case of either them or you.

To our disbelief, the train carried on crawling through the station and never actually stopped. The journey home was just a continuation of the earlier nightmare. The law lost total control of Chelsea that night. The communication cord was pulled repeatedly, leading the coppers to finally tell us that if we acted like animals, then we'd be treated like animals. With that, they turned all the lights out. It didn't change a thing. We seemed to be stopping every ten minutes as the cord was pulled again. It was then that I realised I hadn't eaten the chocolate I'd bought in Birmingham. I reached into my pocket only to find that the once lovely chocolate bar was now a sticky, sodden mass. At that point, two things happened. The lights went out yet again and we immediately went into a tunnel. We were instantly thrown into total darkness. In the gloom, I could just about make out the outline of some kid's steel rimmed glasses. He was sitting against the window opposite me towards the left. I don't know why, and I still don't know why, but I chucked the ball of chocolate straight at him. It hit him full in the face. As we got out of the tunnel the light came back on again. The kid was going mad! In fact, he now looked like Al Jolson in *The Jazz Singer*. He immediately went for one of his mates. To my disbelief, they started scrapping with each other. I just sat there. It was bloody amazing. He never thought of the possibility that it could have been me. I quickly stuffed my hands into my Harrington as they were covered in the stuff. Somehow, I was never blamed for this act. I think a mixture of his fury and everybody else pissing themselves laughing at him, got me off the hook.

Do you know, about five years later, I met 'chocolate head' again at Chelsea and he was still blaming his mate for that incident. I just said, 'Yeah, that was a real shitty trick he pulled on you!' He agreed, and said, 'I knew that you'd never do a thing like that.' I nodded in agreement and tried to look sincere.

And so, the journey went on and on. Gallagher turned to me and said he was busting for a piss but that he was too scared to leave the compartment, as by this time the Chelsea nutters had taken to throwing fireworks into the corridor. I said to Gallagher, 'Don't be so bloody ridiculous – you'll have to go!' He finally plucked up the courage and made his way to the toilet. When he came back, we wedged the door shut so that he couldn't get back into the compartment. Within seconds, bangers were being thrown at his feet from the Chelsea supporters in the other compartments. We were weak with laughter at him hopping from foot to foot; he looked like he was auditioning for *Riverdance*. Gallagher was pounding on the door begging for us to let him back in. Eventually, we took pity on him and let him back into the refuge of our compartment.

Now, with the distance of all the intervening years, it seems like a bit of a laugh, but at the time I remember feeling terrified of what else could go wrong and wondering if I'd ever see home again.

A few hours later, when the train stopped again for the umpteenth time, one of the kids in our compartment opened the window and said that there was a station up ahead. It was Apsley. That was my home town station since moving from London to the suburbs. 'Quick, Neil, you can get out here! Jump out, while we're stopped.' I looked out of the window. The station platform was a good few hundred yards away, and it would mean crossing some live rails. I actually opened the door, when a copper shouted, 'Shut that bloody thing and sit down, you stupid little bastard!' Thank God he did. With the way the day had been going, I'd most probably have been hit by the London to Manchester express as soon as I'd put my head out of the door. Either that, or I would've fried alive on the live rails.

At last, we pulled into Euston at about 11.30pm. The journey home had taken six and a half hours. It should have taken two at the most. I said my goodbyes to Gallagher and Kevin, who lived in London, and arranged to meet them the next week. Thank God, the Chels were at home!

On the train back to Apsley, I got talking to a Coventry supporter who had that day been to watch his team play at Crystal Palace. We were getting on well and having a good chat. It was nice to talk to someone who on the surface seemed sane. 'Hang on a minute,' he said, 'I've got something for you in my holdall.' With my luck that day, I half expected him to pull out a machine gun, pull a black mask over his head and announce to the rest of the train, 'I'm from the Palestine Liberation Army! I now control this train! Take me to Cuba!' Thankfully, he just handed me a can of beer. We then went on to have a nice, civilised drink, and relaxed for the rest of the trip, my faith restored.

After a two-mile walk back from the station, I eventually arrived home, well past midnight. The welcoming committee, i.e. my mum and dad, were gunning for me. My old man went totally ballistic. 'You can't be trusted! You're never going again!' Etc., etc. When he calmed down, I told him what had happened and that it wasn't my fault. Suddenly, the penny dropped with my dad. He told me that it had been on the national news that night about the way the Birmingham supporters had tried to derail a 'football special'. And so, grudgingly, I was forgiven. My dad, taking pity on me, said that I could go to the next away game if I wanted to. To tell the truth, at that moment, I wished that my dad had stuck to his guns. The thought of another away trip didn't exactly fill me with a nice warm feeling. At that moment, if I'd had my way, I don't think I would ever have left Stamford Bridge again – and I mean ever.

Chapter 21

Decline and Fall

WHAT IS it like to watch your team turn from one of the most powerful sides in the land into a joke? Not pleasant, I can tell you. Three years after Chelsea lost the 1972 League Cup Final to Stoke, they were relegated to the Second Division. The deterioration at the club was rapid and brutal. The year after that defeat at Wembley, we finished 12th, and the year after that we limped home in 18th place. The drop into the bottom three in 1975 was not unexpected and the defeat to Spurs at White Hart Lane was decisive, as it was between us and them as to who stayed up. The 2-0 defeat practically sealed our fate.

Travelling back on the tube, I asked Gallagher what he would do to the referee if he could get his hands on him. Now, this referee happened to be Jack Taylor, who had refereed the Holland v West Germany World Cup Final, so let's just say that he was somebody that was really well known and was considered to be the finest referee in the land. He had disallowed two Chelsea goals that day, and as far as I can remember, at least one of them should have stood. Gallagher replied to me, 'I'd wring his fucking neck.' Add in the fact that Jack Taylor was about 6ft 4in and built like a brick shithouse, this would have been some task. I said to Gallagher, 'Well, that's handy because he's sitting next to you!' Gallagher's face drained of all colour because, yes, in fact, there was Mr Taylor. Unbelievably, the match referee of such a hostile game between two deadly rivals was actually sitting in our carriage, full of Chelsea supporters – something that, today, would be absolutely unbelievable. Gallagher, rather meekly, turned back into his seat and carried on reading his programme, never once making eye contact with Mr Taylor.

The decline of the club really began in May 1972 when the East Stand was pulled down to be replaced by a brand-new edifice. Overnight, the Bridge became a building site. It was fully two years before the new stand was opened. The knock-on effect of building the new stand and the massive bust-up between manager Dave Sexton and a host of players, which included the idols of Stamford Bridge, Ossie and Huddy, was instrumental in bringing the club to its knees.

Gone were the days of free-flowing football. They were soon to be replaced by turgid indifferent performances. Not to put too fine a point on it, we had become absolute shit. The ground was a dump. Behind the foundations of the new stand, you could see a graveyard, just behind the railway lines. And to top it all off, the players of both sides had to get changed in a portacabin. After a time, teams would come to the Bridge and give us the complete run-around. I've lost count of how many occasions I stood in the Shed with Gallagher, watching Chelsea disappear in ever decreasing circles. The ignominy of watching some scally, northern bastards, dancing with joy down at the North End as another goal hit the back of our net, was sickening.

There were two moments in those years that summed it up for me as to just how far we had fallen from grace. The first was a home game at the Bridge against Charlton in December 1975. By that time, we were entrenched in mid-table of the Second Division. Yet again, it was the same old story; we were all over Charlton, dominating the game, but twice they caught us on the break, both goals coming from near-post headers, from almost identical corners. Again, we had fallen to the classic sucker punch.

In the second half, Chelsea laid siege to the Charlton goal and eventually we pulled one back. Chelsea continued to pour forward and were rewarded when Ian Britton hit a brilliant overhead kick into the Charlton net to make it 2-2 with ten minutes left. And then came a moment that I will never forget. With five minutes left, Charlton were just kicking the ball anywhere to relieve the pressure. On this occasion, the ball was hit downfield, deep into our half. It sailed over Ron Harris's head and suddenly he was aware that the Charlton centre-forward, Derek Hales, was on his shoulder. However, Chopper had a head start on him and tried to shepherd the ball back to Bonetti, who was racing off his line. In that moment they both hesitated. It was a fatal error. They collided with each other and Chopper, unable to get out of Bonetti's way, jumped straight into the keeper's arms. They looked like they were hugging each other before they crashed to the ground. The ball ran loose to Hales who, unable to believe his luck, calmly side-footed the loose ball into the back of our net.

Both Chopper and the Cat are Chelsea legends, but at that moment they just lay there looking like Laurel and Hardy. For Gallagher and me, that was enough. We just turned around and walked out of the ground. It totally summed up what we had turned into – a laughing stock. On the walk back home to Victoria (I was staying at

Gallagher's that night), we hardly said a word. To have dominated a game in that way, only to throw it away with a goal that should have belonged in the Keystone Cops, was devastating.

Worse was to follow in February 1976. On a Saturday, we'd lost 3-2 to Crystal Palace, then a Third Division side, in the fifth round of the FA Cup. Again, we were 2-0 down at half-time. Again, we pulled the game back to 2-2, only to lose to yet another late goal. It was becoming a nasty habit.

Shortly afterwards, we were at home to Hull City. It was probably one of the most miserable nights I've ever spent at the Bridge. We'd gone from a ground packed with 50,000 against Palace, to barely 9,000 for that night's game, which was yet another mediocre occasion. The ground was like a graveyard. There was a furious north-east wind blowing and on top of that it was sleeting. Standing there in that meagre crowd was an experience that plumbed new depths.

Hull had come for a point. They hardly mounted an attack all night. But the moment that encapsulated Chelsea's decline was when the ball was centred by Britton. His cross fell straight at the feet of Bill Garner, who found himself completely unmarked in their penalty area. He must've only been about 12 yards out. The goal was at his mercy. At last, we were going to break the deadlock. But somehow, he managed to take a swing at the ball, completely miss it, and ended up in a tangle of his long gangly legs. He contrived to back-heel the ball straight to a Hull defender, who quickly set up his side on a counter-attack. There was total silence, followed by the jeers of the crowd, and sadly, there was laughter. And Gallagher and myself found ourselves laughing with them.

The team, who I had idolised, were now a joke. The team that in the previous ten years had played in four major cup finals, countless semi-finals and finished third in the First Division, were now down in the bargain basement.

Chapter 22

Blue Remembered Hills

I OFTEN think about those fields and those times. It was a total of just five years, from 1970 to 1975. I mean, what is that? Five years is nothing really. But there is something magical and strange about those formative years. So much happened to us in that short space of time. We started off as boys and through that brief passage, became young men. Those fields are now being built on and when I saw that, it choked me. A reminder that nothing is forever. I still dream about going down to the fields, even to this day. On quite a few occasions, I'm the only one knocking for the others to come out to play, only to be told that they have grown up and moved on. It's easy to couch the past in a golden glow but I know, having said that, those were halcyon days.

Of course, we all had worries common to teenagers: school exams, friendships or lack of them, girls, how we would fit in with everybody else, but those five years were a lifetime for us. The strange thing is that at the age of 20, we all felt that we were too old to be going down to those fields and to be playing in a street team, and one by one we all joined Sunday league teams, which ended those days at the fields.

Now it seems ludicrous that we felt that way, but in those days, there was social pressure to get a steady girlfriend and settle down. Today, that is totally different. I once worked with a bloke who proceeded to tell me all about his tacky, sordid love life. At the end of this rather tedious story, he concluded by saying, 'I know it's all a bit of a mess, but I'm only 29.' Unsurprisingly, I found his words hard to take.

I still think of those days on a regular basis, and the smell of freshly cut grass in the spring reminds me of those fields after we came out of the hibernation we had endured for those long winter months. To finally find we were free to go to those fields every night was a liberation. Go past any playing fields today, even in the height of summer, and they are empty. Kids now seem to live their life on a phone and in front of a computer screen, which in my opinion is very sad. Four hundred friends on Facebook are no substitution for friends formed through a shared experience.

I could go on about this forever, but I think I'll leave it to A. E. Houseman's words from *A Shropshire Lad* – I think this says it all:

> 'Into my heart on air that kills
> From yon far country blows:
> What are those blue remembered hills,
> What spires, what farms are those?
>
> That is the land of lost content,
> I see it shining plain,
> The happy highways where I went
> And cannot come again.'

Chapter 23

Loathe Story Part 1 – Spurs

THERE IS no doubt there's a team that all Chelsea supporters of my generation hate, and that is Spurs. I have two nephews who are Blues, and whilst they don't like Spurs, their vitriol towards them is nowhere near as intense as mine. I suppose it's the age thing. For most of the time that they have been following Chelsea, Tottenham have been no threat. It's only recently that they have become more of a challenge.

Like all Chelsea supporters of my age, it all started with the 1967 FA Cup Final. Although I was only 11 when we lost to them at Wembley, the bitterness towards them from that match was still emanating around Stamford Bridge when I started going to games regularly in the 1968/69 season. The mere mention of the name Spurs at the Bridge created pathological hatred. That they had denied us our first cup win was a scar inflicted upon us that will never heal.

When we won our first FA Cup in 1970, that did lay a lot of ghosts to rest. We had come so close, so many times. In fact, in 1965, '66 and '67 we had played in three consecutive semi-finals at Villa Park, only to lose on two occasions before beating Leeds 1-0 in '67 with Tony Hateley's goal. What made that first FA Cup-winning season so sweet was also the fact that Spurs had endured a miserable season, finishing mid-table, plus Arsenal, despite winning the Fairs Cup, also finished nowhere in the league, having been hammered 3-0 home and away by us that year.

The following season, Spurs finished above us in the league and won the League Cup. But we topped that by winning the European Cup Winners' Cup, beating Real Madrid, no less. The year after, in 1972, we got the better of them again, this time in the League Cup semi-final, beating them 5-4 on aggregate after a titanic struggle. It was a great way to pay them back for the 1967 final. I have to say, on my visits to White Hart Lane, I have always been shocked at how the Spurs supporters get on to their own players' backs. Sometimes it was brutal. I remember Alan Mullery got terrible stick for the fact that he wasn't Dave Mackay.

Another thing that sets them apart from the supporters of other teams is their belief that they have a divine right to win things. You know, the 'glory, glory' farce. My God, you'd have to watch Pathe News to actually see Spurs winning the league.

Over the years we have dumped Spurs in the brown stuff on numerous occasions; for example, the 16-year unbeaten run in the league – OK, I know they beat us in the 2008 League Cup Final, a game in which we didn't turn up, but we'll draw a veil over that. Unbelievably, they also bring out DVDs of the rare occasions that they've managed to get the better of us, not realising that that makes them look inferior on every level.

A day that will live long in all Chelsea supporters' memories is 19 May 2012, as we not only won the

Champions League that night, but actually denied Spurs a place in the competition, as we earned the right to defend our trophy as the holders the following season. So, despite Spurs finishing two places higher than us in the league, we had again ruined their dreams. Add in the way we handed the title to Leicester in 2016 by drawing 2-2 with Spurs, in a game that mirrored every Chelsea supporter's feelings towards them. And finally, to bring it right up to date, when we won the Premier League in 2017, who finished runners-up? You guessed it. And whilst I would admit that Spurs's Harry Kane is a fine player, I would like to end by saying, 'Cheer up, Harry. Why the long face?'

Chapter 24

Loathe Story
Part 2 – Liverpool

NEXT TO Spurs in my list of loathing are Liverpool. Now, during the 70s and 80s they didn't really bother me. Basically, they were winning everything, and we were in the middle of the wilderness years but, it always seemed that every time we played them, especially in cup games, we actually managed to beat them.

No, it's their hankering for past glory, since their trophies dried up – that's what really gets me. The media are to blame for this as well. When we won the Champions League in 2012, our coverage on Sky Sports on the Sunday for the trophy parade, was miniscule compared to the coverage they received back in 2005, after Istanbul. Their deluded stance on their club is not shared by the supporters of other teams and it is a shame that the media can't seem to quite grasp that. And, as for their fans, that is another myth.

I went to Anfield back in the day and let me tell you, there was no warm welcome from the Scousers. I remember being covered in spit after Liverpool's fans were waiting for us at Lime Street Station. In August 1972, we played Liverpool at the Bridge and they beat us 2-1. In fact, they went on to take the league title that year. I was with my mate, Gallagher, and after the game I got the train back to Euston from Fulham Broadway whilst he was going to get a bus back to Pimlico, near Victoria, where he lived. At the bus stop, he was jumped by a group of Scousers who gave him a right kicking. At the next home game against Manchester City I was shocked to see that he had taken quite a beating. He had two black eyes and his lip had been split quite badly. Now remember, they had actually won that game and even that wasn't enough for those friendly, lovable Scousers.

And of course, they have other charming habits, i.e. the 'warm pocket' which basically is the practice of pissing in somebody's pocket, probably somebody standing in front of you, when you can't get to the toilet. And then there's the charming habit of throwing bags of shit at rival fans. Add in the fact that they also threw bricks at the ambulance that was taking Man United's Alan Smith to hospital after he horrifically broke his leg at Anfield, and you start to see that behind the façade of their self-perpetuated image, lies a heart of darkness.

Now, they would counter, how about Chelsea, you're no angels. And they would be right. But we have never painted such a false picture of ourselves. And please don't get me started on the professional Scousers, such as Phil Thompson, who always seems to me to be about one outburst away from being sectioned. And then there's Mickey Quinn on *Talk Sport*, who actually said on the radio during the week of our Champions League win against Bayern Munich, that Chelsea were a plastic club with no history. I would like to remind the rotund windbag that while they went 30 years without winning the league (yes! 30 years), we won five Premier League titles. I was watching Liverpool TV a few years ago (also known as the History Channel) when Peter Hooton, the lead singer of The Farm, remarked that after we had beaten them in the 2008 Champions League semi-final at the Bridge, he was approached by Chelsea fans asking him, 'How do we celebrate? We just don't know how to celebrate.' I must add, that I was only watching this joke of a channel because it came free with my TV package and it was always good for a laugh. But the crowning moment was when Joey Jones was being interviewed on their channel. As well as being a Blues legend, Joey had actually played for Liverpool before coming to his senses. He proceeded to say that the Chelsea fans were the most loyal, die-hard fans of any club that he had played for. The interviewer's face was a picture. You could hear a pin drop in the studio. The likes of Spurs and Liverpool have never suffered in the way that we did, and I would love to see how they would have handled their respective clubs going through so many lean years.

It is also interesting to note that before Bill Shankly took over at Liverpool at the turn of the 60s, they had been perennial under-achievers, always threatening to win something, but missing out on the big prize. They were, in fact, in the second division when he took over and had never won the FA Cup – now who does that remind you of? No one can deny them their history of winning titles and European Cups, but that was a long time ago. It also gives me great delight that we have constantly rained on their parade. Yes, I know that they beat us in two Champions League semi-finals, but the controversy of the ghost goal that they scored in the first semi-final has been extensively analysed and there has been no final conclusion. And I'm sure that if that had happened at the Bridge, the goal would never have stood.

Just like 2012, when we won the Champions League, their name was on the trophy that year in 2005. Not even a plague of locusts would have stopped them. It also gives me a warm feeling that we have knocked them out of the Champions League a couple of times. We've also beaten them in both FA Cup and League Cup finals, and surely the icing on the cake was our 2-0 win at Anfield in 2014, that in reality ended their hopes of winning the title. I was almost sick at the thought that we would never hear the end of it if they had actually managed to win that title. Sky Sports would have gone into overdrive. What a terrible thought. The moment that Steven Gerrard slipped and let Demba Ba in to score was one of the sweetest moments in all the years I've supported the Blues. It even led to Gerrard having his contract terminated by Teflon.

The nightmare that I always dreaded became a reality last year when Liverpool faced Spurs in the 2019 Champions League Final. The thought of the Scousers winning the Champions League was bad enough, but the thought of Spurs lifting the trophy made me physically sick to the stomach. The idea of them parading the highest honour in club football through the streets of north London, followed by their endless bragging, was something that I could not begin to contemplate. We, the Chels, are the only London team ever to have won the Champions League, and long may that continue.

No need to worry, Liverpool beat Spurs comfortably 2-0. The thing is, that on the night, Liverpool were bloody awful, but somehow Spurs in their own special way, were even worse. They completely bottled it and surrendered meekly. I've got to admit that I actually supported Liverpool in that final. For me, it was the lesser of two evils. In fact, I felt almost like a condemned prisoner being asked whether he would prefer to be hung or shot when he was executed. So, Liverpool winning was bad enough, but if Spurs had taken the trophy – unthinkable.

All in all, it was a good week. Chelsea thumped Arsenal 4-1 in the Europa League Final and Spurs reverted to type, yet again, by promising so much and delivering so little.

Chapter 25

The Long Hot Summer of 1970

THAT SUMMER of 1970, after Chelsea's first-ever FA Cup win, is one of my treasured memories. I bathed in the glow of the Blues' triumph during that six-week school holiday. My mates and I played endless games of football down at the fields, interspersed with Subbuteo tournaments and playing the board game, Wembley. Poor old John Clarke didn't win a single game of Wembley that summer. No matter how high the number he threw on the dice, it always ended up in failure. We thought he'd broken his duck when it was between him and Chris Espley in the final. John threw a six. Surely the cup was his? But no, Chris then threw a six. John couldn't believe it. So, they had to throw again. John in his impatience, then threw a five only for Chris to take the trophy by throwing a six. All of us were in hysterics. John, though, failed to see the joke and promptly stormed off, muttering bitter curses under his breath.

We also had a Subbuteo league and cup competition that summer, where we played the games at our various houses. All the matches kicked off at the same time at each house, and we actually used to phone each other's houses with half-time scores and final results. How sad. It's a great shame that something like this activity is now lost to the distant past.

I was a serious Subbuteo player, and had won various school tournaments. I had my own pitch mounted on chipboard with fencing all around and a scoreboard, and my grandad even made me a royal box, just like the one at Wembley. Consequently, I won the league and cup double easily. Poor old John Clarke suffered again during this tournament, this time at my hands as I thumped him 21-0. Chris Espley designed the winner's trophy, which was a plastic disc inscribed, 'Subbuteo League Champions 1970'. I kept my two discs for years. It was strange though that Chris, who finished runner-up to me in both league and cup, seemed to have a more elaborate disc for finishing second than I had for coming first. I wonder how that happened?

Typical of the cruelty of kids of that age, Chris even designed a plastic wooden spoon with the words inscribed on it, 'The League Was Lost By ...' In this case, the booby-prize went to Tim Burke. Safe to say, I shouldn't imagine it was ever proudly displayed in any part of his home. In fact, it most probably found its rightful place in the dustbin.

Of course, there was also the small matter of the 1970 World Cup finals that summer. After watching that magnificent Brazil team that year, we tried to emulate all of their fantastic pieces of skill down at the fields. Sorry to say, most of them ended up in total failure. But I remember one night when we tried out their free-kick routine. John Clarke played the role of Tostao and stood on the end of the wall alongside the defenders. The idea of putting an attacker with the defending side was something that had never been seen in this country before. I, of course, played the part of my brand-new hero, Roberto Rivellino, who possessed a thunderous shot as well as a Mexican bandito moustache. It was a simple trick. I ran up and blasted the ball towards John Clarke. At the last minute, John got out of the way, leaving a gap in the wall and my shot hit the back of the net before the goalie moved. In that instant I firmly believed that I was, indeed, Rivellino himself, and that I was part of that great Brazilian side that went on to take the World Cup that year.

That routine from Brazil was such a simple idea, but in a country like ours, where Sir Alf Ramsey's ideas had been deified since the 1966 World Cup win, it was unheard of. I've got to say that Ramsey's philosophy for our game was pretty dreary. It was all quite stale and functional. Flair players were not encouraged in Ramsey's kingdom. Consequently, players like Ossie, Rodney Marsh, Tony Currie and our own Alan Hudson, found themselves very much on the outside of Ramsey's England set-up. Time and time again, these hugely talented, skilful players would be left out as Ramsey faithfully stood by the players who had won the World Cup for him in 1966. It was a culture that eventually cost Ramsey his job in the spring of 1974, after the failure to qualify for that year's finals in Germany.

So, that great Brazil team of 1970 is one that blokes of my generation remember with huge fondness. They showed that there was nothing wrong with individualism and that skilful players could be moulded into a collective unit.

In a ground-breaking summer for football in 1970, there was, of course, the introduction of the ITV World Cup panel that was devised by Jimmy Hill to challenge the BBC's domination of coverage of our national game.

The BBC's rather dull, flat effort seemed more at home in the 1950s, complete with presenters with short-back-and-sides haircuts and off-the-peg suits. It was all very staid and English. Jimmy's plan was revolutionary. The ITV panel consisted of Jimmy himself, Malcolm Allison, Derek Dougan, Pat Crerand and Bob McNab. The whole thing was hosted brilliantly by the late, great Brian Moore. No one had ever seen anything quite like it. They had fierce arguments amongst themselves. They wore the colourful clothes of that era and they even smoked on air – Jimmy Hill and Brian Moore with their pipes, and of course, Big Mal (Malcolm Allison) smoking his huge cigars. It was just like watching four normal blokes arguing the toss over their pints in the local boozer. Such was the intensity of their debates, albeit with good humour, I'm pretty sure that there must've been some drink taken when they were off air, during the advert breaks. In a single move, Jimmy Hill had changed the way that football was viewed in this country.

In fact, that ITV panel of 1970 is the unquestionable direct ancestor of Sky's *Soccer Saturday*. But, no matter how good Jeff Stelling and his guests are, nothing will ever eclipse Jimmy Hill's brilliantly inspired idea of putting such a cast of opinionated, colourful characters together, back in that summer of 1970.

But, how quickly those summer days went past. Days that were full of hedonism and football. Looking back, it was a once in a lifetime experience of one halcyon day followed by another. But as Bruce Springsteen insightfully said in his song, *Glory Days*, a paean to lost youth:

'Glory days, well, they'll pass you by

Glory days, in the wink of a young girl's eye.'

I think the Boss summed it up far better than I ever could, so I'll let him have the last word.

Chapter 26

A Warped Vision

ONE THING that really annoys me is the way that those days are portrayed in film and TV. Every male actor depicting the 1970s nowadays seems to have a droopy Zapata moustache topped off with an ill-fitting long-haired wig, and of course, bell-bottoms with the whole sorry mess being finished off with ridiculous stack-heeled shoes. And of course, all the girls are wearing hot-pants, crocheted sleeveless cardigans and knee-high boots. It seems that every witless director falls into the same trap of turning those days into a sad pastiche of what they were really like.

And don't get me started on the way football is represented by all those luvvie actors and directors. Take *The Damned United*, which I suppose is one of the better attempts. Apart from Michael Sheen's spot-on portrayal of Brian Clough and his infamous 44 days in charge of Leeds United, the rest of the film descends into parody. The re-enactments of the actual matches look fake, to say the least, and smack of being made by people who have no empathy or understanding of the game at all.

One of the worst examples of this genre is a film made back in the early 1980s called *Yesterday's Hero*, starring Ian McShane and Adam Faith. McShane's character is the stereotypical washed-up pro, who has taken to drink and is now plying his trade in non-league football. Paul Nicholas takes on the role of the pop-star chairman of an up-and-coming third division team. (I wonder where they got that idea from?)

For some reason, Nicholas, in his infinite wisdom, decides that McShane would be an ideal replacement for their star centre-forward, Jake Snatcher (yeah, that's right, Jake Snatcher!) who had tragically broken his leg. When team manager, Adam Faith, violently disagrees and protests that it would be madness to take a risk on an old has-been, the dim-witted chairman suggests that one of their up-and-coming young players might be a good alternative. Faith replies with the classic line, 'No, we can't do that. He'd shit his pants.' Unbelievable!

So, consequently they're left with no choice but to go with the dipso, McShane. Strangely, no one seems to have noticed that McShane himself has what looks suspiciously like the beginnings of a pot-belly, and already looks like he's pushing 40. Then, there is the ludicrous sub-plot of the pop-star chairman, Nicholas (clearly based on Elton John who was the Watford chairman at the time), and, of course, the American girl singer, Cloudy Martin, who naturally falls in love with McShane. The nadir of the whole fiasco is perhaps the scene where Paul Nicholas and Cloudy Martin (played by B-lister Suzanne Sommers), perform their latest chart-topper, a song so bad that the word 'execrable' is now included in the Oxford Dictionary as the definition of this turgid tune. The staggeringly awful song, *I Got You, You Got Me, We Got Us*, is beyond belief. Of course, this steaming pile of brown stuff is at the top of the charts and is met with rapturous applause by the adoring crowd.

And so, the story plays out with McShane going on to score the winning goal in the FA Cup Final after his team 'The Saints' recover from 2-0 down to win the cup 3-2. Why they were called The Saints soon becomes strikingly apparent when you realise that the director of the film has used footage of the 1979 League Cup Final between Nottingham Forest and Southampton, intercut with poorly-judged shots of McShane waddling around the hallowed turf. Think about it. What is Southampton's nickname? Why of course, it's The Saints. How convenient. You can now use all of that footage of Southampton fans at Wembley with all their flags and scarves held proudly aloft. Job done.

Yesterday's Hero also featured that great, old, venerable actor from many British films, Sam Kydd, playing McShane's dad. There was even a cameo from John Motson, who does his best impression of a plank of wood whilst interviewing the victorious Saints players after their win in the FA Cup semi-final. Of course, the pop-star chairman, Paul Nicholas, is thrown into the team bath by the joyous players. I reckon to this day, that Nicholas wishes they'd thrown him in head-first and drowned the poor sod to put him out of his misery.

Now, you may ask, who was responsible for the screenplay? It's a question I asked myself at the time. Well, it was none other than that purveyor of sleazy crap, Jackie Collins. I suppose she must have been the obvious choice really, with her vast knowledge, understanding and insight of the game. This abortion of a film puts the Sean Bean wet-dream project, *When Saturday Comes*, almost into the category of an arthouse film. Having said all of this, I love *Yesterday's Hero*. I used to watch it on video with one of my mates on a yearly basis. It was the ultimate guilty pleasure. It was great fun watching this complete load of bollocks, with a few cans and a few cigars. It really is the gift that keeps on giving.

But surely, the football movie to end them all is *Escape to Victory*? Where do you start? The terrible acting? And I'm not just talking about the ex-pros playing the prisoners who are forced into playing against a team of Nazis in the Second World War. Somehow, perhaps it might even have been blackmail, the brilliant Michael Caine was involved in this ludicrous piece of nonsense. Both he and Max Von Sydow looked like they'd dialled in their parts. Caine, who was approaching his 50s at the time, spends the whole film bawling out nonsensical instructions to his team-mates, whilst he gasps and plods his way around the pitch. But the scene that takes the biscuit is right at the end of the film when the crowd break down the barriers, allowing the team of prisoners of war to escape with them.

If you look closely, and I have, somebody in the crowd seems to be wearing a 1970s tracksuit top. How strange. I never realised that such apparel was around in occupied Europe during World War Two.

Unbelievably, the director of this fantasy was none other than John Huston. Yes, the same John Huston who directed *The Treasure of the Sierra Madre*, and *The African Queen*, amongst many other classics. It really does beggar belief. I know Huston had a reputation for being a hard drinker, but surely nobody could be that drunk? But, once again, *Escape to Victory* has, perversely, almost become a perennial favourite of mine. I always seem to watch it whenever it's shown on TV. I think I might even own a DVD of the film. I suppose the best way of summing it up is that *Escape to Victory* is the visual version of a scab;

you know you shouldn't pick it, but somehow you just can't stop yourself.

Back in those days, there was also the trend of actual players appearing in cameo roles in various TV programmes. I remember watching *The Mike and Bernie Winters Show*; they were a sort of very poor man's Morecambe and Wise. This particular episode featured Ossie and Charlie Cooke in a really lame sketch about football. To say the whole thing was an embarrassment is an understatement. I could feel my face turning bright red and watched the whole debacle through my fingers that were covering my face. It was excruciating.

Then of course, there was the Esso Blue TV advert that was shown in November 1972. It featured the Chelsea squad singing their hit single, 'Blue is the Colour', with adapted lyrics to fit the subject matter. It also had the cartoon Esso Blue Man leading the squad in their droning sing-song. Now, this advert was mentioned in the previous home game's programme, telling you what time and what channel it would be aired on. Remember, the *Mike and Bernie Winters* fiasco was still clear in my mind. I just couldn't face it all again, seeing my heroes making complete doughnuts of themselves. So, a couple of minutes before the advert was due to come on, I ran out of the front room, opened the back door and stood in the garden whilst the macabre event took place. This was, as I said, November, and it was bloody freezing out that night. I stood there for a good five minutes past the scheduled time of the advert, just in case the programme had got the timing wrong. When I eventually returned to the front room, my dad said that it wasn't that bad, albeit with a smirk on his face. Of course, in time I saw that advert many times and, to be quite honest, it wasn't as bad as I had imagined. It was, after all, just another example of how football and show business have always been strange bedfellows.

I suppose, as time moves on, TV, film and plays about that era will become progressively worse, as most of these forms of media seem to be produced, directed and acted by a collection of Julians and Jocastas, fresh out of film and drama school. Yes, the girls will still be called 'dolly-birds' and look like Adrienne Posta from the film *Up the Junction*, and all of the blokes will have a passing resemblance to Robin Askwith from those old dreadful 'Confessions of …' films.

However, I did see a play on TV back in those days that was in itself an absolute rarity. It was an accurate, spot-on depiction of Sunday League football. It was written by Jack Rosenthal and was called, *Another Sunday and Sweet FA*. I tracked it down a while ago on YouTube, and no, my memory had not played tricks on me – it was still brilliant. Jack Rosenthal seemed to have a real insight into the game which, to this day, remains a rarity. It centred around a Sunday league match situated in the north somewhere, and it was played out with the interaction between the beleaguered referee, Mr Armistead, played by David Swift, and the various players of both sides. This being the Sunday league, the players came in all shapes and sizes. It really did look totally authentic, even down to the sight of players having a quick drag on a fag on their way out of the changing rooms. Of course, this was also followed by another crafty smoke at half-time. Then, after the final whistle had blown, they would all be off down the pub to completely nullify all the good exercise that they had put themselves through for 90 minutes.

The narration, rather cleverly, is the referee's stream of consciousness as he makes comments to himself about each of the team's skills, or should I say, lack of them.

What with all the constant sniping from both sides, the exasperated ref abandons the game. He is, however, eventually persuaded by both captains to carry on. Yet, within a few minutes, the back-biting from both sides starts again, pushing the referee to breaking point. This is brilliantly illustrated when, in the last minute of the game, the referee himself meets a cross from the right and heads the ball into an empty net. The players of both sides are dumbfounded as the referee runs away, punching the air in celebration. The picture then freezes on the image of the referee celebrating his goal. After all that dog's abuse that he had received, he did what I expect many referees at that level would like to do, and inflicted the ultimate revenge on two teams of hapless idiots.

At that level of football in the Sunday league, if you wanted to secure a place in the team every week, then who you drank with was vitally important. It was a necessity to get into the right clique and stick close together with your cronies to make totally sure that you were in the line-up every Sunday, come hell or high water. I've got to say, I struggled with this culture of back-slapping bullshit, and therefore had to suffer from time to time dubious omissions from the side. I remember going on a club trip to Clacton one day. It was a bloody nightmare. The usual suspects were half-cut before we got halfway to our destination, and then proceeded to hit a local pub on the seafront where they remained for the rest of the day. Now, please don't run away with the idea that I just used to sit in the corner nursing a Britvic orange and lemonade. I liked a drink. I was in a band at the time, and that band in all honesty, was a confederacy of drunks, myself very much included. But as I discovered, there were hard drinkers and then there were also knuckle-scraping morons, like the members of the team that I played for. With my mates, we got quietly drunk and didn't really bother anyone else. But no, the motley collection of fuckwits from the football team inflicted their gruesome activities on anyone within spitting distance. The journey home was a joy to behold, with endless, moronic sing-songs. The strange thing is, all of this lot, to a man, were fucking hopeless at football. They really were the epitome of all that was wrong at that level of the game. You won't be surprised to know that I stuck it out for a couple of months, before making my escape.

One final word on that cinematic classic, *Yesterday's Hero*. I did some digging online and found out that the football adviser on this masterpiece was none other than Frank McLintock, Arsenal's 1971 double-winning captain. Oh, Frank, what were you thinking of? You showed about as much knowledge of the game as a house brick. Mind you, the climax of the film centred around a third division club, The Saints, overcoming a top-flight side to win the cup. So, suddenly, it all fell into place. Of course, Frank had first-hand knowledge of this scenario when he skippered the Gunners to their 3-1 defeat against third division Swindon in the 1969 League Cup Final. Now it all made perfect sense. Yes, in retrospect, Frank was the perfect man to go to.

Chapter 27

Nemesis

JUST BEFORE the first game of the 1972/73 season, I got a call from Steve Gallagher saying that he'd met some blokes where he was working as a volunteer at Shelter, and they'd said that Steve and I could go along with them to the away games the next season. Big deal, I thought. Why couldn't we just go to the games on our own? No, Steve said, it'll be good. They're all about 25, 26 years of age. Steve said they would look after us and show us all of the tricks involved in following Chelsea away.

Straightaway I had my doubts. They were ten years older than us and being 17 in 1972 really did mean that you were just 17. The majority of boys in those days were definitely still boys. Secondly, I quite enjoyed it being just me and Steve going to the games. As it turned out, in the long run, I was right. From the offset, they ripped the piss out of us from start to finish. They were, to a man, smart-Alec Chelsea boys; all of them clued up and streetwise. Both of us were shit scared to open our mouths. Just one slight mistake by Steve or me and they were all over us like a rash.

Steve, because he was so in awe of their leader, Ian, couldn't see what was going on right in front of his face. Down the years, I've realised just how much Steve and I were influenced by Ian. He was such a piss-taking, arrogant, and highly intelligent sod. He had an answer for everything. He seemed so self-assured and possessed a lexicon of insults that both Steve and myself still use to this day. He was also a raging Nazi elitist who had no time for people that he considered were not his equal. He was good looking and well dressed and always had sharp haircuts. I hated him from day one.

Going to the games became less fun for Steve and me. How could you enjoy yourself when you were terrified to open your mouth, for fear of half a dozen of your elders making you feel like a total prat? As the season wore on and Chelsea's fortunes nose-dived, some of them stopped coming to the games, and that suited me right down to the ground. Not Ian, though. He was there until the bitter end. Still, Steve couldn't see that Ian was actually looking down his nose at us all of the time. Steve considered Ian to be his new best friend. To have a mate ten years older than yourself and cool into the bargain, was a prized possession.

One day, I chanced my arm and started taking the piss out of Ian and began questioning him on why he wore a beard. I said that I'd heard that growing a beard was a sign that you were insecure and also sexually repressed. It was most probably a lot of old toss, but I thought I'd give him back some of his own medicine when I made these savage comments to him. Ian just replied, 'Yes, Neil. You're probably right. I am insecure, and I must admit I might even be sexually repressed, but at least I've got a beard to hide behind. All you've got are your pimples and your fucking, pathetic bum-fluff.' I just stood there, speechless.

Steve laughed hysterically. I could've gladly killed both of them right there and then.

However, there was one moment of light throughout that season of darkness, when Ian got his just desserts. It was before one of the early-season away games. I was to meet Steve and Ian and his cronies outside St Pancras Station, before we travelled up to Derby for the game that afternoon at the Baseball Ground. I can distinctly remember that they were quite late turning up. When Steve and Ian arrived, they both looked worse for wear. It turned out that they'd been on the piss the night before and were still feeling the effects. Ian seemed to be carrying something under his arm. On closer inspection, I could see it was a suit. What the hell was Ian carrying a suit for? Steve said, 'We've just got to drop this in to a dry-cleaners.' And then went on to tell of the hilarious evening they had spent together which had ended with them going around the back of the Army and Navy Stores, to have a piss. Unfortunately, Ian had pissed down himself and soaked the front of his trousers, hence the need for the dry-cleaners.

I traipsed a few steps behind them to a dry-cleaners further along the Euston Road. Ian went up to the counter and handed his suit over to the assistant. Seeing that I was at the back of the shop, I couldn't quite make out what was going on, but I could see that there seemed to be some sort of trouble. I moved closer to the counter so that I could get a good listen. Let's get one thing straight, the woman serving Ian was bloody rough, and I mean rough. She held Ian's trousers up and said, 'What's this stain then?' For the first time since I'd know him, Ian was lost for words. The assistant then proceeded to sniff his strides and said, 'That's piss!' Ian, somewhat red-faced, came back with, 'I can assure you that it's not!' But his protest was weak and feeble. It was obvious to everybody that he was lying. She sniffed his trousers again. 'Yeah, I'm right. It is piss. We charge extra if garments are soiled.' Neither Steve nor myself made a sound but inside, I was screaming with laughter. In total silence, Ian collected his ticket and we made our way out of the shop to the station. And if my memory serves me well, it was never, ever mentioned again by either Steve or myself, so fearful were we of Ian's wrath.

I don't know about Steve, but for me it was a moment of sweet revenge. Ian went with us to most of the games that season. All in all, I found it a bit of a strain. At 17, you just want to be 17. It was almost your divine right to be a bit childish at that age and to feel free to act like a total prat. You didn't need some bloke, ten years older than yourself, watching every step you made, waiting for you to make yet another goof-ball comment that he could use against you.

Then, as suddenly as it had started, that time with Ian came to a close. After the home game with Spurs in April 1973 (another wretched 1-0 defeat), I had the dubious honour of traipsing back to Euston with Ian. Because Steve lived just around the corner from Victoria Station, I was left alone with my nemesis. As we travelled up the escalator, we talked about the Chelsea performance that night, which had been, in all truth, abysmal, and about what had become of that great team that we had seen just a few short years ago. Now, the club seemed to be in freefall.

When it came to the time for me and Ian to part ways, I said to Ian, 'See you at the next home game.'

'No, you won't.' he replied. 'I've had enough. That lot are only going one way – and that is down.' He then proceeded to go into a diatribe about Chelsea's shortcomings, but to tell you the truth, his words were an absolute joy to hear. This would be the last time I'd ever have to set eyes on that fucker. Somewhere between those torrents of words that he spewed, he mumbled, 'See you around, sometime.' And that was it. Neither Steve nor myself ever clapped eyes on him, or heard from him again. Strangely, Steve never mentioned getting a call from him. I just said to Steve that that night at Euston Ian had seemed fed up with the way Chelsea were heading, and it seemed to be the right time for him to get out.

Sadly, Ian was right. Within two years, we were in the Second Division. I suppose that must've given Ian a nice warm feeling inside, that he'd jumped ship at exactly the right time. As for Steve and me, we were bound, like all the other Chelsea faithful, and stayed on board with the Blues and sunk without a trace, just like our beloved team.

Chapter 28

Webb of Deceit

NOW LET me get one thing straight. I know that everybody talks about other people behind their backs. It's just human nature. But Steve Webb took this practice to another level. I think it was something all of us were aware of, but being nice, typically English boys, our natural reserve kicked in and we kept Webby's barbed comments to ourselves. That is until one night down at the fields.

We were sitting on the grass bank after our final game of the evening. Somehow, we found ourselves talking about Webby, due to the fact that he had gone home early. I don't know how it started, but the subject of his bitching about everyone spread like wildfire and became the hot topic that night. As it turned out, he'd been talking about all of us behind our backs on a regular basis. It was then that I had the idea of taping him, in secret, so we would have a record of exactly what he thought about us.

Now, there's no doubt that I got off lightly, as I was to take on the role of the interviewer. Michael Parkinson's chat show was a hugely popular programme in those days. It was the first US-style chat show in this country. *Parkinson* was always packed with all the A-listers from Hollywood. So, for one day only, I would indeed become Parkinson himself. Therefore, I would miss out on the chance of hearing what Webby thought about me.

So, on Thursday, 1 June 1972, the day after Ajax had beaten Inter Milan with two goals from Dutch maestro Johan Cruyff in the European Cup Final, Kevin and I made our way to John Clarke's home where we had set up a secret microphone hidden in an empty playing card box. John had a very large house, so we had hidden the tape recorder behind the settee that he had on his spacious landing. What Kevin was doing there, God only knows, as his job would be to do nothing more than hide in John's bedroom, eavesdropping whilst Webby inevitably insulted him. John's role was to sit next to me as my stooge while I questioned Mr Webb.

I can't really remember how we managed to get Webby to come around to John's house that day but, somehow, he gladly accepted the invitation. He was totally ignorant of what we were up to. His naivety was almost unbelievable. How he didn't cotton on that something was afoot, I still can't quite believe to this day, as I even had a crib sheet next to me with the questions I would be putting to him. I told John that on no account must he show any sign of guilt on his face about what we were up to.

After Webby had settled down on the settee on the landing, it soon became apparent that he was in a very chatty mood. Of course, John himself would be exempt, as well as myself, from Webby's bitching, but there were still enough of us within the Avenue regulars for Webby to sink his teeth into. I've got to say that Webby sang like a canary. The tirade of vitriol soon turned into a torrent of abuse concerning his unfortunate team-mates. Sadly, the tape we made of Webby's insults is now lost. However, one spiky slur remains vividly in my memory.

During the interview, I asked Webby what he thought about the fact that Dave and Kevin (the Kevin who was hiding in the bedroom) had clashed heads a few weeks ago whilst challenging for a high ball during one of our games down the fields. Dave and Kevin had both ended up in a crumpled heap on the deck, looking dazed and confused, with blood streaming down their faces from the gashes in their foreheads. What, I asked, did Webby make of this incident? He just sat back on that settee, with a knowing smirk on his face, and said, 'They were acting.' My jaw dropped. He then went on to say, 'They'd seen something like that on *Match of the Day* and they were just putting it on.' 'What about the blood?' I enquired. But no reply was forthcoming from Mr Webb. All I got in return was just another knowing smug look on his face, as if that was the only comment he was prepared to make at this time.

Do you know, we actually had an 'Evening with Webby' night, where everyone – apart from the culprit, Webby – was invited to John's house to listen to the interview. John's mum even provided soft drinks and sandwiches. I've got to say, Webby's diatribe was met with laughter from all of us. There was very little anger, after all, we all knew what Webby was like. We agreed that we could never let on what we'd done to him. I know, I know, it was a sneaky thing to do, but it was great fun. I wonder what Webby would have said about me? On reflection, perhaps it's better that I never, ever found out.

Chapter 29

Bug's Eleven

ON SATURDAY, 22 May 1971, the day after Chelsea had triumphed over Real Madrid in the European Cup Winners' Cup Final replay in Athens, I happily watched England stuff Scotland 3-1 in the Home Internationals at Wembley. That result rounded off a great 24 hours for me. There had been a short break in the build-up to the game as the BBC broke off their coverage for a quick interview with some of the triumphant Chelsea players who had just arrived back at Heathrow. All I can remember of that interview is Ossie and co looking decidedly worse for wear. Their club suits looked dishevelled. They were also all wearing those gaudy, flowery shirts that were the height of fashion in those days. To a 15-year-old boy, they looked extremely tired and worn out. Could they really be suffering from jet-lag after such a short flight? Now I realise that they were half drunk and suffering from monumental hangovers. But such is the innocence that you view your heroes in at that age.

That Saturday night I went round for John Clarke to see if we could get enough of my mates to come out and have a game. Our first stop was to call at Bug's house. 'No, he's not in. You've just missed him. He's gone to play football with his mates against some other team,' his mum told us. Bug was two years younger than us, so we now found out that he had the bloody nerve to have friends of his own, apart from us lot from down the fields. The only other person we talked into coming out with us that night was Tim Burke, accompanied by his little Scottie dog, Sam. There was not much of a game we could have with just the three of us and it was a well-known fact that although Sam would sit faithfully behind the goal at those fields whenever Tim played, he was more of a cricket fan!

Then I had the brilliant idea – why not go and watch Bug's team, seeing as we were so few in numbers? We quickly went back to Bug's house and asked his mum where her son's game was taking place. She told us it was being held just near the Catholic church. We were surprised at this as that church was located near the roughest, toughest neighbourhood in Hemel Hempstead. It was largely populated by Irish families, and to us, it was a bit of a no-go area.

Bug's mum told us that they were playing the game at the back of one of the most notorious areas at that time, Ritcroft Street. The match would take place behind the rows of grey, pebble-dashed houses, next to the allotments. '*What the hell*,' we thought. If Bug's prepared to go there, then so will we.

When we arrived on that warm summer evening, we were stunned to find out that the local kids had made their own little pitch behind the allotments, complete with home-made five-a-side goals. Bug looked horrified to see us. After all, we were gate-crashing his own little party, and this was a party that we were definitely not invited to. We announced, with supreme arrogance, that we would take over the team and manage it for that game. Poor old Bug. His face fell. He didn't even have a say in it. I can remember that there were about eight players per side. Now, I fancied myself as a tactical genius, a younger version of Chelsea boss, Dave Sexton. Upon seeing that the pitch which had been created by the local kids was tiny and cramped, I gave the instruction to always go two-up on any opposition player. This meant that one of Bug's team would make a challenge whilst his other team-mate would be lying in wait to cover him. Just by looking at Bug's motley crew, I was not very hopeful, as they came in various shapes and sizes. On the other hand, their opponents looked quite useful when they were kicking the ball around before the game got under way.

I don't think Bug appreciated us standing behind him as he kept goal, but there was nothing he could do about it. My plan of doubling up on the opposition was working well, as the far-superior local kids were finding it difficult to find space on that postage-stamp sized pitch. Bug's team were trailing 1-0 at half-time. Not a bad result seeing that they'd been under the cosh for most of the first half. We gave them a quick half-time team talk and told them that the plan was working well. Although I have to admit that they were not the most talented bunch of footballers I'd ever seen, somehow they managed to stick to those tactics to the letter.

Halfway through the second half, Bug's team equalised. John, Tim and I celebrated like we'd just seen our team score the winning goal in the cup final. Even Sam, the little Scottie dog, was running around in circles, barking his head off!

At full time, Bug's mob had got away with a 1-1 draw, despite being battered for most of the game. A good result, you might think. But no, the offer of playing extra time by their opponents was accepted by Bug and his team-mates. John and I told them they were mad. Take the draw, we said. They'd been lucky to get away with that result. But Bug and his cohorts were having none of it. Almost inevitably, the local kids then went 2-1 up in the first few minutes of extra time. Poor old Bug looked really sheepish as he picked the ball out of the back of the net. We gave him a right mouthful. 'What did we bloody tell you, you twat!' That, and other endearments, were thrown at Bug's team. Unfortunately for Bug, as he was the goalkeeper and therefore nearest to us, he copped much of the dog's abuse that we dished out. But to give Bug's team credit, they stuck at it and unbelievably hit an equaliser in the last few minutes. From then until the final whistle, we serenaded Bug and his heroes with the song, 'La-la-la, Bugsy FC,' to the tune of T Rex's 'Hot Love'.

It had been a great night. The 2-2 draw was a brilliant result for Bug and his mates. Then one of the local kids shouted out, 'We'll play you back here next week.' Before Bug could agree to this, I told the other team, 'Oh no, we'll play you at our place, this time.' It was a fatal mistake.

When the game was played on the following Sunday on our full-sized pitch down at the fields, our two-up, doubling-up tactic didn't work at all, as this time Bug's opponents used the wide open spaces to their advantage and ran out comfortable 4-1 winners. It was the first and last blunder of my short managerial career. Halfway through that game, John and I had lost interest in poor Bug and his beleaguered team and actually started kicking our own ball around on the upper pitch.

Poor old Bug. His team were being torn apart by their opponents. At half-time, Bug ran up the grass bank that separated the lower field from the upper field. 'What should we do?' Bug pleaded. Such was the callousness of youth, my reply was cutting. Poor old Bug, 3-0 down without any hope or any talent, received my pearls of wisdom with tears in his eyes. 'Don't ask me,' I said. 'You've got yourself into the shit. Why don't you get yourself out of it?' Both John and I found that hysterically funny as we laughed right in Bug's face. He cut a desolate, lonely figure as he made his way back to his outclassed team-mates. John and I didn't give it another thought and just carried on with our kick-about. Strangely, Bug never asked us to manage his brave little band again ... I wonder why?

Chapter 30

West Ham Away – 1970 – Part 1

JUST BEFORE the start of the 1970/71 season, I saw an advert in a football magazine for a cup winners' scarf that Chelsea were bringing out. I sent off my postal order as quickly as possible. When I received the prized scarf, even though it was incredibly hot that evening, nothing would stop me from wearing it down to the fields that night. I've got to tell you, I was burning up as I approached the fields but there was no way I was taking that bloody scarf off. Once again, I could bask in the glory of that night at Old Trafford in April when we had won the cup.

It was about a year later that the wearing of the silk scarf around your wrist came into fashion, something I could never bring myself to do. No, I was a traditionalist. For me, just the blue and white scarf worn under my Harrington or Crombie was the look I was going for. There was also the trend of having your programme in the back pocket of your Levi Sta-Prest, a display that almost dared someone to try and nick it. Or there was the alternative of carrying the programme tightly rolled up in your hand. Don't ask me why. Such was the swagger that was required in those days in supporting the Blues.

I was on holiday on the Isle of Wight with my family when the 1970/71 season kicked off and learnt that Chelsea had lost the Charity Shield match at Stamford Bridge, which was contested between the FA Cup winners (Chelsea) and the league champions (Everton). The Blues had lost the game 2-1. A pretty meaningless result, you might think. But not to me. Again, I went into a stroppy teenage sulk. To think we'd lost at home to that lot. I mean, they were only the league champions, after all. What made it even worse was that Everton captain, Alan Ball, strutted around in that game wearing his Hummel white boots, something that back in those days was considered to be outrageous. Although the result of losing to Everton was totally meaningless in the scheme of things, that was no consolation to me.

On the Sunday, I was still annoyed that my dad had refused my pleas about going back to our B&B early the previous evening to watch the game on *Match of the Day*. He had said, 'What do you want to watch that for? They lost the bloody game, anyway! We're all on holiday. Give it a sodding break, will you!'

However, when I saw photos of the game the next day in the newspapers, I noticed that there was something slightly different about the badge on the Chelsea shirts but, after carefully scrutinising the photos, I still couldn't quite make out what the difference was. So, I went to a toy shop in Ventnor High Street and bought myself a magnifying glass, such was my desire to solve the mystery. Upon closer inspection through the glass, I at last discovered the answer. Chelsea had added the symbol of the FA Cup next to the crest of the lion with 1970 emblazoned under the cup.

Unfortunately, in those days there was no chance of getting one of these as this was long before the culture of replica shirts came into fashion. No, it was only the Chelsea players who would have the honour of proudly displaying our brand-new club badge.

That FA Cup emblem was only worn for one season. It was replaced the following year after our European Cup Winners' Cup Final victory over Real Madrid with two stars either side of the lion denoting our two successive cup wins. Yet again, that shirt was unavailable to supporters. What an opportunity clubs missed in those days, when you think of how much revenue is created with the craze of replica shirt sales today. Now the clubs change both home and away kits every season. It really is the gift that keeps on giving.

Actually, I can't think of any other club in the country before Chelsea that had used different badges to celebrate their success. I'm pretty sure that the Blues broke new ground with this innovation. Of course, the idea of adding stars to the badge was not new in the international game. I believe that the Brazil World Cup-winning team of 1970 were the first team I ever saw to adopt this idea. Now, of course, it is everywhere. I think the England national team were one of the last teams to have won the World Cup to actually add a star to denote our 1966 win, when the archaic FA finally gave in to public pressure to adopt some form of recognition of our achievements.

The only downside of the badge that Chelsea started wearing in the 1971/72 season is that the Blues continued wearing those two stars on their shirt long after the glory days of the early 70s were nothing but a distant memory. I think it was finally replaced in the 1986/87 season by chairman, Ken Bates, who wanted to herald a new era by introducing his own Chelsea collection. It was a disaster and for quite a few years after that, we wore a collection of revolting kits. And then, of course, there was the new club badge designed by Mr Bates himself. There was no exception in the opinion of his effort; it was universally hated by all Blues fans. Thank God the club finally saw sense when the traditional lion crest of the Earl of Cadogan's arms was reintroduced before the 2005/06 season. There's one thing I can't stand, and that's when clubs start messing around with traditions that I feel should always be honoured.

We travelled back from the Isle of Wight on the opening Saturday of the 1970/71 season, when Chelsea were at home to Derby. I decided not to find out the score, on the off-chance I might be able to watch the game that night on *Match of the Day*. So, in effect, if I were lucky, it would almost be like watching the game live. How I resisted the temptation not to phone one of my mates to find out the result, I'll never know.

We arrived back home that Saturday at about half past seven, so I had just under three hours to wait for the highlights to be shown. It seemed an eternity until *Match of the Day* came on. I was in luck. Chelsea v Derby was one of the main games. Unfortunately, it didn't start well for the Blues. The defence, which had looked shaky the previous week against Everton, left John O'Hare, Derby's centre-forward, completely unmarked in the box. It was a chance that he accepted gratefully as he smashed the ball past Peter Bonetti. I feared the worst. It was a weird experience watching that game at home that night. I found that I had to curb my mouth, otherwise my mum and dad would have come down on me like a ton of bricks. At half-time, the Blues were still trailing 1-0. Then, in the

second half, much to my relief, Ian Hutchinson scored
with two headers, the second being a typically brave effort
from Hutch as he got on the blind side of a defender and
headed into the roof of the net from a narrow angle, to give
Chelsea a 2-1 win. I tried to restrain myself to just jumping
out of my seat in celebration, but let myself down rather
by shouting out, 'Take that Cloughie, you fucking twat!'
There were icy stares from both my mum and dad, but I
think they could understand my joy. It was our first win of
the new season, against a really useful Derby County side.

I couldn't go to the next home game, which was against
Everton (again), and which ended in a disappointing
2-2 draw. It became an even poorer result in retrospect,
when Everton, who at the time were the First Division
champions, ended up in mid-table after a miserable season.

The next game up was West Ham away. I was
determined to go, despite the fact that my cousin, Carol,
was getting married on the Saturday of the game. All my
family would be in attendance and my sister was going to
be one of the bridesmaids, so it was a big family day. My
mum and dad and my aunts tried in vain to persuade me to
go to the wedding, which was being held at the Elephant
and Castle, where I had lived in London. Aunt Gladys,
who was the bride's mother, tried her hardest to change
my mind. But she may as well have been talking to a brick
wall. I was going to Upton Park, come hell or high water.

It was arranged that I would travel back to the wedding
reception after the game, and then stay at my aunt's
overnight until the Sunday. So, on that Saturday morning
of 22 August 1970, I travelled together with my family
on the train up to Euston. And then, there was a parting
of the ways. They all headed off for their tediously dull
wedding whilst I started out on my journey to West Ham.
Being slightly naïve or just plain stupid, I wore my blue

and white scarf on the way to Upton Park, a decision that would come back to haunt me.

I've got to say that the atmosphere inside Upton Park was loud and hostile. I eventually found a place to stand, just where the players would emerge from the tunnel. It was a brilliant view. I remember that there had been a scare story in the papers that day that some nutcase, who said he was a sniper, had phoned the police to say that he planned to shoot members of the England squad, following their failure to retain the trophy in that summer's World Cup. The following week, Arsenal captain Frank McLintock was added to the sniper's list. Now, as McLintock was a Scottish international, this seemed somewhat strange. Perhaps the assassin thought that he'd throw him in as part of a job lot.

Of course, Bobby Moore, the England captain and Geoff Hurst, the hat-trick hero of the 1966 World Cup Final, both played for the Hammers. It must've been no easy task for those players to run out that day at Upton Park with the threat hanging over them. Of course, Chelsea also had Peter Osgood and Peter Bonetti, who had both been members of that England squad in 1970. Bonetti personally must have felt that he would be the prime target in any telescopic sight, seeing as he was carrying the can for England's World Cup quarter-final defeat against West Germany. Bonetti had been a late replacement for the regular England goalkeeper, the great Gordon Banks, who had been laid low with a mystery stomach bug on the day of the game. It all looked very shady on the part of the Mexican nation, as there was no love lost between their country and ours. In fact, in that game, the whole stadium, apart from the few England supporters, were rooting for the West German side. In just a few short months Bonetti suffered both sides of the game. He had been a hero in both the cup finals against Leeds and was probably one of the main reasons why the Blues lifted their first FA Cup. But just a couple of months later, he was labelled as the man who lost England the World Cup, after conceding two soft goals to the Germans.

I shall never forget the horrendous abuse that Bonetti received as he ran up to take his place in goal, in front of the Arsenal supporters massed on the north terrace at the beginning of the following season. To a man, they chanted 'Bonetti lost the World Cup.' It was harsh, very harsh.

It wasn't until years later that England manager Sir Alf Ramsey's dubious tactics were called into question. With England leading 2-0 with 20 minutes to go against the Germans, he took off a couple of key England players, including Bobby Charlton, no doubt to rest them for the semi-final which now seemed almost guaranteed. The Charlton substitution was easily the most damaging. He had dominated the midfield that day, causing West Germany's Franz Beckenbauer to shadow him. Finally, free from having to man-mark Charlton, Beckenbauer found the space to advance and scored the first goal for the West Germans, which suddenly swung the game back in their favour. Though Bonetti put in many fine performances for the Blues after that nightmare in Mexico, I always felt that he carried the stigma of that defeat against the Germans for the rest of his career.

As the players emerged from the tunnel that day at Upton Park, I was pleased to see that Chelsea were wearing their change strip of yellow shirts, blue shorts with the yellow stripe, and the yellow socks. They looked great. I was looking forward to seeing our new signing from Millwall, Keith Weller, who had cost us £100,000 just a few months earlier. You've got to remember that £100,000 was a big fee in those days. Charlie Cooke and David

Webb, who had been heroes in the FA Cup Final victory against Leeds, had both started the season in patchy form. So Weller replaced Cooke on the wing that day. They were big boots to fill. Irish full-back, Paddy Mulligan, came into the defence in place of Webby. The raucous noise inside Upton Park, where you were practically on top of the players, was easily the most hostile and fervent atmosphere I'd ever experienced. It was reaching fever pitch by the time West Ham kicked off. Jimmy Greaves was in the West Ham line-up, after signing from Spurs earlier that year. Unfortunately for Jimmy, his stay at the Hammers was cut short by the fiasco at Blackpool the following January, when he and a few other West Ham players decided that the best preparation for their cup tie against the Tangarines was to get drunk the night before. West Ham, consequently, were hammered 4-0. Not long after, Jimmy departed, and his career was over.

Back at Upton Park, West Ham were playing like men possessed, and, what with the crowd roaring them on, it was more like a cup tie than an early-season fixture, albeit a London derby. I suddenly realised, to West Ham, we were a big scalp. They had the FA Cup-holders on the back foot and rooted firmly in their own half. It was no surprise when West Ham took the lead after 11 minutes with a powerful shot from the edge of the box from Bobby Howe. I can tell you now, it's not a nice experience to be the only silent figure amongst hordes of home fans celebrating a goal. It got worse a short while later when West Ham went two up, the second goal being scored by Hammers legend, Geoff Hurst. I stood there with my blue and white scarf around my neck in a sea of claret and blue. Chelsea's defence, which had looked shaky at the start of the season, was now looking dangerously vulnerable every time West Ham attacked. It was a relief when the referee blew the whistle for half-time. I know we were two goals down, but it could've been a lot worse.

That was a long ten minutes, waiting for the second half to start, surrounded by loads of east Londoners prematurely celebrating what they were sure was going to be their day. As soon as the second half kicked off, Chelsea seemed to have more purpose about them and within minutes, Weller had pulled a goal back. Now it was West Ham's turn to look uneasy as the yellow-shirted Chelsea players laid siege to the home team's goal. Whatever manager Dave Sexton had said to his team at half-time seemed to have woken the Blues up. An equaliser now seemed on the cards, and it duly arrived when Weller grabbed his second goal of the game to make the score 2-2. Now it was my turn to celebrate, though it was strange to be the only one jumping up and down, surrounded by silent, glum West Ham fans.

Chelsea continued to press for a winner, but West Ham held firm. In fact, the Hammers had the best chance late in the second half when the normally lethal finisher, Greaves, hit his close-range effort straight at Chelsea keeper, Bonetti. I was relieved when the final whistle blew and that the game had ended in a draw. It was not very nice being surrounded by the home fans, who were hoping and praying that my team would get stuffed. I was looking forward to my first home game of the season at the Bridge the following week, against Arsenal. It would be good to be in the majority rather than the minority as I had been that day at Upton Park. There were lots of stony-faced West Ham supporters around me, so I decided to let the crowd empty out of Upton Park, before I made a move.

Though the points had been shared that day, there was no doubt that to the majority of West Ham fans, there was the feeling that their team had thrown away the game after leading 2-0. A draw in those circumstances almost tastes like a defeat. On the other hand, I, and I should imagine most Chelsea supporters, were relieved that we'd managed to come back to get a draw in a game where we'd had to endure an early onslaught from the home side who were being roared on by the partisan Upton Park crowd.

Chapter 31

West Ham Away – 1970 – Part 2 (The Loneliness of the Long-Distance Runner)

AFTER ONE-AND-A-HALF seasons of going to watch the Blues on a regular basis, I mistakenly thought that I was fast becoming almost a veteran at finding my way through the dangers and pitfalls that came with supporting the Blues. I thought I'd learnt the ways of keeping safe at the games, especially away from home, and that's why that day I had my scarf hidden under my jacket as I made my way out of Upton Park. There was no way that I would want to be involved in anything like what had happened outside Euston Square after the Man United game in March 1969, where my friends and I had been jumped by United fans.

So, I tried to blend in with all the disgruntled West Ham fans making their way back to the tube station. Again, there was a heavy police presence everywhere that day as it was no secret that the West Ham following and

Chelsea's following didn't really see eye to eye on most things. In fact, I found West Ham and their mob to be the most bloody terrifying supporters of any team in London. Their hardcore, which congregated on the North Bank at West Ham, went on to become known as the infamous 'Inter City Firm', and then of course there was the Chelsea hardcore of the Shed who would later gain notoriety when they renamed themselves 'The Chelsea Headhunters', sporting black skull and crossbones flags which looked terrifying. So, it was something of a relief when the tube train finally pulled out of the station and I made my way on the journey to the wedding reception at St Barnabas Hall in the Elephant and Castle, which was just down the road from the Imperial War Museum.

Sometime on that journey, when the train had virtually emptied and the last few West Ham supporters had left the carriage, I made a fatal mistake. *'I'm safe now,'* I thought, *'well away from West Ham.'* What a great idea it would be to get out my scarf that was hidden beneath my jacket, and wear it proudly around my neck to walk into the wedding reception. I would be a hero and revel in the adulation from my uncles who would think to a man, *'Good lad! That's the way to do it. Be proud and wear your colours.'* It was, in retrospect, the mother of schoolboy errors.

When I got out at the Elephant and Castle tube station, I took the bumpy ride up in the ancient, rickety old lifts they had back then, and got on to street level, emerging into what was a lovely late summer's evening. As there are a few different exits to the Elephant and Castle tube station, I quickly got my bearings and then started out on my way from that station to walk to the wedding reception. I was looking forward to basking in the glow of the admiring looks I would get from my uncles, all of whom I held in the highest regard. There I would stand, one of the boys, showing no fear of West Ham's notorious supporters.

Then things started to turn very dark. The first thing I heard was a shout of, 'Get that Chelsea fucker!' I looked behind to see who on earth they could be screaming at. Then I saw three or four blokes who were a few years older than me, wearing claret and blue scarves. In that moment, time stood still. Then they charged towards me and I was under no illusion that they wanted to shake my hand and say, 'Well played old chap. A draw was a fair result.' There was no doubt in my mind that they intended to give me what is commonly known as a 'right kicking'. There was no choice. I had to run for it. There is no way to describe the primeval fear that you feel when you're running for your life. It seemed as though my legs wouldn't work properly. It was like one of those dreams where no matter how hard you try, it seems that you are running through quicksand. Now, I was a pretty good runner, part of the district team, but that was for sprinting. This chase was going to go a lot further than 100 yards. All I could hear behind me were the thundering feet and the screams and threats of what they were going to do to me. Luckily, adrenaline kicked in and I seemed to feel no exhaustion. I managed to lose them briefly and ran around a corner and spotted a launderette. I hurtled headlong through the doors. Why? I don't know. If they had spotted me, I would have been caught like a rat in a trap. There were looks of surprise and shock on the faces of the customers in the launderette. Luckily for me, the manageress must have been in the back office or in the loo as there is no doubt I would have been thrown out on my ear if they had been in attendance.

I quickly hid behind one of the washing machines, out of view from the street. I shall never forget the bemused look on people's faces that day in the launderette as they looked on at me, shaking with fear, in my hiding place. I didn't have to look to see if my tormentors were still on my tail. I heard them shouting dire threats as they raced by my temporary sanctuary.

Then the manageress emerged behind me and asked what the fuck I was playing at and said to get the fuck out of her shop. Without a word, I walked silently out of the launderette, but checked both ways when I got to the door to make sure the coast was clear. It was a tremendous relief to see that that bunch of goons must have fallen for my cunning plan. It was only then that I realised how out of breath I was and that my legs were shaking. I stood there for a minute to work out exactly where I was. Luckily, I realised that St Barnabas Hall was just a short distance away. I looked carefully as I turned the corner on to the road where the wedding reception was being held, and there it was, in the shimmering sunlight, St Barnabas Hall – what a beautiful sight.

I could actually see some of my uncles standing outside the hall having a drink and a fag on that fine summer evening. I was about halfway to safety when I suddenly heard, 'There he is!' Once again, I was the prey as my pursuers were on my tail, but they'd left it too late. I raced towards the hall, and safety. My uncles looked surprised to see me hurtling towards them at full speed. 'There he is,' remarked my uncle Ernie as I raced past them into the hall. I then turned around to see my four West Ham friends stop dead in their tracks on seeing my uncles. I distinctly heard Ernie say to the cowardly bunch of goons, 'Where the fuck do you think you're going?' My pursuers looked sheepish at the prospect of taking on my relatives, two of whom had fought at El Alamein against the Germans in north Africa during World War II. How strange that they seemed to back right off. I myself couldn't resist one last parting shot at my tormentors and standing just behind the protection of my uncles, gave them the two-finger salute. One of the West Ham goons shouted back, 'Just you fucking wait!' And that was met promptly by my uncle Arthur moving towards them and telling them in no uncertain manner to fuck off out of it! The last sight I caught of that mob was them skulking back the way they had come. I was lucky, very lucky. It was a stupid thing to do, wearing that Chelsea scarf that day. My foolish bravado had almost got me a right hiding. I would never, ever repeat that mistake again.

'What've you been up to?' someone said. 'Nothing,' I replied. 'It was them.' My uncles just laughed and then my mum came up to me and said, 'Take that bloody scarf off. You can't wear that to a wedding.' No truer words were ever spoken. If only I had heeded the advice she'd given me earlier in the day when she said, 'Don't you think you're pushing it wearing that to West Ham with the reputation they've got?' If only I had listened to her wise words, I wouldn't have had to endure that nightmare chase around the streets of south-east London.

To put a cap on that day, my uncles thought it would be a great laugh later on at the wedding reception to bodily pick me up and shove my head into a huge bowl of jellied eels. Luckily, I managed to break free from their grasp before I was face-planted into that vile-looking, lumpy liquid. I really hated that disgusting concoction.

Now, because this was a London wedding, I settled for the pie, mash and liquor that was on offer. Somebody obviously had had the great idea of ordering an east Londoner's staple diet from the local pie and mash shop. I should imagine that there were quite a few in attendance that night who were sick to death of nibbling on the fancy tit-bits that had been provided.

Londoners would always fall back on that traditional meal of pie and mash. It wasn't just a meal, where I was brought up in the Elephant and Castle, it was a way of life. Even when we went on our yearly trip to Ramsgate, our evenings would invariably end up with the whole family in the local pie and mash shop. I find it strange that that meal which was once the essential diet for lots of Londoners from the east end of the capital, has now become so fashionable. It was a strange sight in Camden Town, where my partner, Trudie, and I lived before moving to the Isle of Wight, to see hipsters with their ridiculous beards and obligatory lumberjack shirts, actually queueing up to be served at our local pie and mash shop. I suppose they thought in their somewhat confused minds, that they were connecting with the 'people' – i.e. the plebs – in eating such working-class food. Still, I'm glad that there's been a resurgence in the interest in what was to a lot of Londoners, a cheap way of filling yourself up for the day.

That night, after the wedding reception, back at my Aunt Gladys's flat, the party carried on. It was a regular thing, house parties on a Saturday night. In the part of London where I grew up, all the neighbours just seemed to accept with good grace the most horrendous noise people were making into the early hours of the morning. I believe it was tolerated, as those on the receiving end would most probably be having their own get-together the following Saturday. My Aunt Gladys's flat was nowhere near as chintzy as some of my other aunts' places. In fact, the décor looked like it was a bit of a hangover from World War II. The main colour scheme seemed to be green, brown and cream. But they did possess that essential piece of any Londoner's home furnishings, the galleon-shaped cocktail bar, complete with optics, in the corner of the living room. All my aunts and uncles loved playing 'mine host' behind those tacky edifices. There was no doubt that it was a sign, in those days, of upward mobility – that you had moved on from the gloomy, austere 1950s and into the bright sunlight of the swinging 60s and beyond.

I was to spend the night in Aunt Gladys's flat, in my cousin Trevor's room. He'd been told that he had to give up his bed for me and sleep on the sofa. He was not very happy. Following the trials and tribulations of that day, I decided to go straight to bed. Now, not to put too fine a point on it, Trevor was a bleeding nutcase. In their infinite wisdom, my Aunt Gladys and Uncle Arthur had bought this maniac a drum kit. God knows what they were thinking of. Trevor then proceeded to give me a demonstration of his drumming skills, which were negligible to say the least. All of this took place whilst I was actually in bed trying to sleep. I was dog-tired and my back ached from all of the standing up on the terraces that day, not to mention being chased halfway around the Elephant and Castle.

The trouble with Trevor was, he never knew when to stop. I was fast running out of patience. Even though Trevor was only a year younger than me, I viewed him as nothing more than a bloody pain in the arse. I can still see him sitting there with that crazed look on his face as he smashed the drums into submission. What made it seem even weirder, was that Trevor had very poor eyesight and wore pebble glasses. Unbelievably, Trevor had confided in me that night that his ambition after leaving school was to become a TV engineer. God help us! How many sets would he have destroyed? The damage across the United Kingdom would have been unthinkable.

After yet another mistimed drum-roll around the kit, he looked at me and said, 'What do you think?' My patience finally snapped, and I shouted back, 'Trevor, I think you should fuck off,' and with that, he threw down his sticks and started muttering, 'I'll tell my mum and dad what you've just said.'

'Fine,' I replied. 'They'll never believe you.'

'Why's that?' he came back with. 'Because they both know you're nothing but a lying little fucker. Now turn the light off and get lost.'

With that he beat a somewhat hasty and sulky retreat. At last, I could get my head down. Of course, almost inevitably, I found sleep difficult as I kept reliving the game I'd been to that day, and the nightmare pursuit that I had later endured on the way to that wedding reception. I'd been stupidly reckless that evening in August 1970 and was lucky that I'd had a bolt-hole to head for. It was a mistake I was determined never to make again. I now realised, after the close escapes I'd had in 1969 and 1970, that both incidents had happened in streets well away from the game. That's where the real danger lay, where stragglers were picked off randomly by marauding gangs of opposing fans. From then on, all traces of my allegiance were well hidden underneath my jacket, only to be displayed once I was safely inside the ground. That is when my scarf would make its reappearance.

However, I've got to admit, I almost got caught again years later. It was 1985 and the Blues had just beaten Arsenal 2-1 at the Bridge. All the goals came in the last 15 minutes with Arsenal flop, Charlie Nicholas, giving the Gunners the lead. Almost immediately, Pat Nevin equalised for the Blues. This was followed quickly by Nigel Spackman blasting home a penalty in the dying seconds, to give Chelsea the win.

Now, I was wearing the white Chelsea away shirt that day underneath my classic 1980s casual jacket. I had decided to queue up after the game to get a couple of tickets for the Spurs match at White Hart Lane the following week. Nothing wrong with that, you might think. The only problem was, the law had kept the Gooners in after their defeat to allow the Chelsea fans to disperse before they let the irate Arsenal fans make their way back to Fulham Broadway. Now, the one thing that the police hadn't taken into consideration was that there were still hundreds of Chelsea fans hanging around buying tickets for that Spurs game, of which, unfortunately, I was one.

As I made my way back from the main entrance to the Bridge, where I had purchased my tickets, I was horrified to find that as I approached Fulham Broadway, I was suddenly surrounded by hundreds of miserable Gooners, who were pouring out of the ground at the north end. The police were escorting them back to the tube station. Somehow, I found myself swept along with them. I quickly zipped up my jacket hoping that the colour of my shirt would be hidden. It was a good job that I'd chosen to wear the white Chelsea away shirt that day instead of the blue home strip. Even so, there was still a slight gap at the top of the jacket where my white shirt was clearly visible. I could only hope that the knuckle-scraping Gooners would think it was just the white collar that they wore on their home strip. I tried not to make it obvious by avoiding almost choking myself by tugging that bloody jacket right up to just beneath my Adam's apple. If that lot had found out that my shirt had the Chelsea lion's crest on it instead of Arsenal's club badge of a cannon on a red shirt, I would be in real trouble. So, I found myself hemmed in with all the Arsenal on the platform and then surrounded by angry, pissed-off Arsenal fans on the tube.

Soon, the song started about their hatred for my team and what they would do to any of their supporters. I could feel cold sweat running down my back. How the bloody hell had it come to this? Trapped in a tin can with blokes who would gladly give me a good hiding if they'd found out what club I supported. And then, to my horror, the train stopped in the tunnel just before we got to High Street Kensington. Those minutes, stuck in that tunnel, seemed endless. I consciously made myself leave the collar of my jacket well alone. I still felt that sooner or later, all the Gooners would spot that I was wearing a Chelsea top. I dreaded one of them clocking me and looking me straight in the eye and saying, 'What do you think you're doing mate? Have you got something to hide?' and then having them rip my jacket open to reveal my Chelsea shirt in all its glory.

It started to get hot in that tube train, with so many people packed in together but was the heat I was feeling generated by all the bodies around me, or my own crushing fear? Then all of the angry Gooners started banging on the windows of the train, such was their frustration at a day that had ended in defeat. To them it must have seemed that there was no sign of their bad luck letting up. 'What the fuck's going on?' and other dire threats were being made about the ineptitude of the London underground before, thankfully, the train jolted a couple of times before moving on again, at long last.

Gradually the train emptied out on its way back to Euston Square. Finally, I managed to get a seat and tried to look as downcast and fed up as the few remaining Gooners in my carriage. Thankfully, yet again, I had got away with it. At long last, it seemed, my experiences all those years ago had taught me something. Displaying your colours to and from a game is never a good idea. If you're trying to make a hero out of yourself by ignoring all of the dangers which that practice entails, just remember how most heroes end up ... dead.

Chapter 32

Last Orders

AROUND ABOUT the time that Chelsea won the Premiership back in 2005, I started receiving emails from my friends from down at the fields, with whom I'd lost touch. I hadn't seen some of them for about 20 years. To be quite honest, I'd instigated the new contact a couple of years earlier, when I tracked down two of my best mates from that time online.

Though I'd enjoyed getting in touch with them, I found it all a bit unsettling to realise just how much we'd all moved on. They, too, were now settled down with wives, kids and mortgages.

I'd been due to meet them both on various occasions but found myself making excuses at the last minute about why I couldn't attend. I think there was that fear within myself, of saying 'do you remember when?' to one of them, only to be met by a blank expression, silently saying, 'What the hell is he talking about?' And so, I did the easy thing – I took the easy way out – and just let all of those arrangements drift. I would just send the occasional email. Nice and easy, I thought.

Then, out of the blue, these emails started coming in. 'Oh my God,' I thought, 'they're arranging a reunion dinner for all the lads I'd grown up with.' The lads who I'd taken my first tentative steps with, into adulthood.

Whereas now you'd go for a curry or a Chinese, back in the 70s it would be a steak dinner at somewhere like a Berni Inn on a Friday or Saturday night – and they intended to retrace those steps. I instantly started to panic. Did I really want to see those mates after all these years? The mates who had been the most important people in my life through those crucial formative days, when we all believed that life was nothing but a feast for all of us to enjoy, only to find out years later that there was in fact no feast; for some of us, there would only be scraps. No, I couldn't face the thought of seeing which of my mates had got fat or who had gone bald, or even worse those who had got both fat and bald.

Chapter 33

Goodbye to All That

AS 1973 turned into 1974, I won the Individual Player League (IPL), which had been devised by Steve Webb. I won the award for playing in goal, which was ironic as I was usually a forward, but had taken on the role of goalkeeper as once again, I had one of the countless injuries I had suffered during my playing days. This injury was caused in February 1971 by a somewhat rotund opponent who landed with full force on the toe of my boot, in freezing cold weather. The nail on my big toe was crushed, bruised and bloodied. This became a long-term problem as a new nail would grow and then become damaged yet again whenever I kicked a ball. Webby initiated the IPL in order to give us something to play for each week. Individual players were awarded two points for a win and one for a draw. That little tournament, played over January and February of 1974, was the zenith of our time playing down at those fields. Things were changing. We were all growing up. Personally, I found myself starting to become chronically bored with staying in on a Saturday night. I felt like a lot of adolescents, that I should be out there doing something, and that life was passing me by. Yes, it's true that we carried on through that spring, playing every Sunday and most week nights, but now there seemed to be other things that were nullifying our passion for playing on those fields; namely girls and drinking.

Suddenly, there was a round of parties on Saturday nights where I found myself nursing a pint of Watney's Party Seven pale ale, trying to get the nerve to approach some unobtainable female. All of this angst that was being played out at the beginning of 1974 coincided with the end of an era at Chelsea, with Ossie and Alan Hudson being sold to Southampton and Stoke respectively, after they had fallen out with Chelsea boss, Dave Sexton. It showed you how far the Blues had fallen; that two of our star players had left us for two unfashionable, mid-table, provincial clubs. But, make no mistake, it was Ossie's departure that cut the deepest. He was the King of Stamford Bridge and still remains so, to this day. Alan Hudson by that time was a pale shadow of the player that he'd been back in 1970. It was the beginning of a dark, depressing era for the club.

Now, our usual Sunday games were being called off on a regular basis due to hangovers and lack of interest. John and I, who had always been the stalwarts, were finding it harder and harder to get the numbers up for a game. The turning point came when I found out that the lads were planning to go on a holiday that year to a holiday camp. I'd been asked back in January if I was interested, but when I heard the dreaded word, 'Butlins' mentioned, I rather quickly declined.

It was in late May 1974 that John told me that the lads' plans had been changed. They were now going to go to Dave Hyde's family chalet at a holiday camp on the Isle of Wight. On the spot, I changed my mind. I'd always loved the Isle of Wight. There were going to be five of us going and it would only cost us the princely sum of £7.50 each for the week! What a result, I thought.

That week we spent at Thorness Bay in June 1974 became something of a legend amongst my mates who went on that holiday. I always felt sorry for the ones who didn't go to the Isle of Wight that year. I can still recall the look of horror on their faces when one of us started recalling those glory days of June 1974. The reminiscing seemed to go on forever and must have been a nightmare for those poor sods who had to listen to our countless tall tales of beer, women and song.

Yes, it's true that we carried on playing down those fields during the summer of 1974, where again we tried to emulate that great Dutch side led by Johan Cruyff, that should have really won the World Cup that year. But instead of going home after our evening game, we would head for the pub. Playing football now, it seemed, was not enough to keep us entertained after the holiday where we all discovered that there was much more to life.

By the autumn/winter of 1974, it was becoming more of a rarity to play down at the fields. To be honest, I was totally pissed off. I still loved going down there and would have carried on. By the spring/summer of 1975, it was all over. Dave Hyde and Steve Webb had moved away, and John Clarke would up sticks in the summer of 1976. This was a big loss to me, as it was John who had been my best mate down at those fields from day one. So, gradually, we all went our separate ways. True, most of us joined the same Sunday league side, and we remained close friends and went on many more lads' holidays. But that magical era, when we all lived in that football-shaped bubble for four wonderful years, was over – gone forever.

In 2002, I was staying at my mum and dad's overnight. During the evening, I decided to get some fresh air and go for a walk. Guess where I ended up? Yes, that's right. I walked over to the fields. Why? I don't know. I suppose it was some form of morbid fascination. As I stood there on that grass bank looking down at the fields where we'd all grown up so many years before, I could still vividly see me and my mates playing the beautiful game. It was a moment frozen in time. Though those friends and those days are long gone, they still live in my mind, and most importantly, my heart.